The Soane Hogarths

CHRISTINA SCULL

SIR JOHN SOANE'S MUSEUM

First published 1991
Second revised edition 2007

Text copyright © Sir John Soane's Museum 2007
Illustrations © Sir John Soane's Museum 2007, except where otherwise indicated

ISBN 978-0-9549041-3-5

Designed and typeset in Albertina by Libanus Press, Marlborough
Printed by BAS Printers, Romsey

Title page: *Chairing the Member*, from *An Election*, showing the frame
(Photograph: Geremy Butler 2006)

The details are taken from the following paintings:
p. 1 *An Election* I
p. 10 *An Election* I
p. 30 *A Rake's Progress* VI
p. 50 *An Election* III
p. 64 *A Rake's Progress* III
These are shown at actual size

Contents

Preface to the Revised Edition 2007

Since this volume was first published in 1991, the celebrity status of the Soane Hogarths has continued to grow. In 1997 *A Rake's Progress* featured in a special exhibition at the Museum together with the precursors and successors of Hogarth's great social satire. The crowds flocked to the Gallery and the catalogue sold out within weeks. In 2001, General Election year in Britain, *An Election* was given its own show which proved a soothing tonic for a nation weary of politicians and their antics. This exhibition then toured to the Laing Art Gallery in Newcastle, the first time the paintings had ever travelled outside London.[1]

The continued popularity of the paintings is a testament to Hogarth's genius both as an artist and as a storyteller. The scenes from each series are packed full of pungent detail, humour and pathos. The characters are plucked straight from the streets and taverns of 18th-century England, and the streets and taverns are there too, together with their smell and noise. Tom, the Rake, is shown drunk, amid the clamour of a Covent Garden brothel, the room permeated by the smell of candle-smoke and sweat. The first painting in *An Election* depicts a similar scene, except this time the orgy is a culinary one, enhanced by lavish helpings of beer, wine and oysters, as the politicians attempt to seduce wavering voters. Both the jokes and the moral messages are as pertinent today as they were in Hogarth's time and the paintings continue to amuse, fascinate and inspire. The spirit of William Hogarth is very much alive and well in 21st-century Britain.

It is fitting that the first revised edition of this volume should appear in the year of the greatest Hogarth exhibition to date, an extravaganza at Tate Britain featuring both sets of Soane's Hogarths. All this would amaze and delight Hogarth who struggled throughout his career to achieve just recognition as a painter.

I would like to thank Geremy Butler, who took the photographs of the twelve Soane pictures used in this new edition. All the images are of items from Sir John Soane's collection unless otherwise stated. Special thanks are also due to Lynn Roberts and Paul Mitchell for their help in describing the frames of both series.

I am grateful to my colleagues Helen Dorey, Will Palin and Sue Palmer who have revised Christina Scull's original text extensively to incorporate new material published on Hogarth in the last twelve years.

TIM KNOX
Director of Sir John Soane's Museum
December 2006

Foreword to the First Edition 1991

The Soane Museum's twelve paintings by William Hogarth are justly famous and a high proportion of the visitors who come to the Museum do so chiefly in order to see these pictures. Such visitors often ask for a booklet with information about the paintings but no such publication has hitherto been available and the present offering is intended to meet this need.

Recognising the need, I invited Christina Scull, who has for many years presided over this Museum's Library and Drawings Collection, to undertake the task of preparing this illustrated booklet, providing a brief account of the Soane's Hogarths and explaining what is to be seen in each picture. Miss Scull has fulfilled her task admirably within the agreed framework; if the book is longer than anticipated, Hogarth must be held responsible!

We should particularly like to thank Elizabeth Einberg, Assistant Keeper of the Historic British Collection of the Tate Gallery and Dr David Bindman of Westfield College, London University, for advice they have given on various points. The staffs of the British Library, the Royal Library at Windsor, the Victoria and Albert Museum, and the Print Room at the British Museum were also most helpful. The twelve paintings were photographed at the Tate Gallery in 1987 after they had been cleaned there for showing at the *Manners and Morals* exhibition. The photograph of *Chairing the Member* in its frame was taken by Geremy Butler.

The publication of this work was made possible by a grant from Mobil North Sea Limited.

PETER THORNTON
Curator, Sir John Soane's Museum

The Soane Hogarths: An Introduction

On 27 February 1802 William Hogarth's series of eight paintings *A Rake's Progress* was sold at Christie's and bought for 570 guineas by Eliza Soane on behalf of her husband, the architect Sir John Soane (1753–1837). Joseph Farington records in his diary on the 28th '. . . Soane called on me. – He purchased the Rakes Progress by Hogarth yesterday at Christie's for 570 guineas. – Mrs Soane was the bidder & was commissioned by him to go to £1000. – He means to put them up at Ealing' (a reference to Soane's country house, Pitzhanger Manor). Twenty-one years later, on 23 June 1823, Soane purchased the four paintings of Hogarth's *An Election* at Christie's, the Auctioneer declaring 'As returning officer I have the honour of declaring that John Soane Esq. is the successful candidate in this warmly contested election.'[2] Soane records their purchase in his Notebook: 'At Christie's, Bought Hogarth's Elections [sic] 1650 Gui[nea]s, Dined alone, Drank Tea Bedf:[d] Pl:.' He no doubt appreciated the concluding comment in the *Gentleman's Magazine* report of the sale: 'However, by becoming master of this series, Mr. Soane has evinced a gallantry of spirit which places him among the most prominent virtuosi of the day.' This book describes these two famous series of paintings, and the engravings made after them, but first we should look at Hogarth himself before discussing the pictures in detail and examining why Soane wished to acquire these paintings.

1. Christopher Hunneman, portrait of John Soane, *c.*1776, oil on canvas
2. The Picture Room at Sir John Soane's Museum, 13 Lincoln's Inn Fields, with the two series of Hogarths hanging on the walls. The room was redecorated in 1988 in accordance with its appearance in Soane's time (Photograph: Richard Davies for HG Magazine, Condé Nast Publications)

William Hogarth: Life and Work

William Hogarth (Fig. 3) was born on 10 November 1697. His family lived at various addresses in the Smithfield area of the City so William grew up surrounded by the turbulent life of a great metropolis that was to play such an important part in many of his paintings and engravings. His father, Richard, had moved from the North to London eleven years before, but success eluded him; he made a precarious living as a schoolmaster and from writing Greek and Latin text books. A new project in 1704 was Hogarth's Coffee House where Latin was spoken so that Gentlemen might practise the language. About four years later the failure of this project led to Richard being confined in the Fleet Prison for debt, though he seems to have been able to evade the severest confinement and live in an adjacent house within the precincts. He remained there until 1712 when an Act of Parliament freed certain classes of debtors. This unhappy period made a great impression on the young William and, indeed, Scene VII of the *Rake's Progress* series (p. 45) shows the Rake imprisoned in the Fleet for debt. Penury meant that Hogarth's father could not afford to pay for young William to continue his education or to apprentice him to an established painter; the best that could be done was to apprentice him in 1714 to an engraver of silver plate, one Ellis Gamble. Much of the work was repetitive and mechanical, but nevertheless this beginning in the world of engraving was crucial to Hogarth's later career.

William did not complete his apprenticeship but in 1720 set himself up as an independent engraver, producing modest items such as trade cards. He was able to attend the St Martin's Lane Academy, began to produce satirical prints and eventually obtained some commissions to illustrate books. While he was at the Academy he would have received instruction in the formal aspects of painting and drawing and would have had the opportunity of drawing from life. In his *Autobiographical Notes* Hogarth records that he was not entirely satisfied with the academic method of teaching by copying but found that for him the best method was 'the retaining in my mind's Eye without drawing upon the spot whatever I wanted [to] imitate . . . [I] soon found by experience this was the readiest and least laborious way for by this means my studies and my Pleasures went hand in hand & the most striking incidents that presented themselves to my view ever made the strongest impressions on my memory.' He also wrote 'Subjects I consider'd as writers do – my Picture was my Stage and men and women my actors who were by Mean[s] of certain Actions and express[ions] to Exhibit a dumb show.'

Many of his early prints were concerned with satirizing contemporary events such as *The South Sea Scheme*, an allegorical attack on the greed of investors,[3] or *Masquerades and Operas*, an attack on contemporary taste for foreign entertainment; in the late 1720s he also began painting topical subjects such as John Gay's successful production of *The Beggar's Opera*. Sir James Thornhill, one of the leading history painters of the time,

3. William Hogarth, *Self Portrait*, c.1735–40, oil on canvas. (© Yale Center for British Art, Paul Mellon Collection, USA / The Bridgeman Art Library)

4. William Hogarth, *The Wedding of Stephen Beckingham and Mary Cox*, 1729, oil on canvas. (The Metropolitan Museum of Art, Marquand Fund, 1936 (36.111). Photograph © 1982 The Metropolitan Museum of Art).
This is a good example of one of Hogarth's Conversation Pieces and it is interesting to compare this formal wedding group with the satirical treatment of the wedding in *A Rake's Progress* (see page 41)

took an interest in the young Hogarth, though their relationship cooled for a time when Hogarth married Jane Thornhill, in 1729, without her father's consent. In 1735 Hogarth started a new St Martin's Lane Academy which, together with the nearby Old Slaughter's Coffee House, was a meeting place for a group of artists who opposed the rigid restraints of Palladianism and were influenced by the delicacy and elegance of French painting, especially as practised by Watteau and his followers. This group, which did much to introduce the Rococo style to England, though in a less extravagant form than on the Continent, included the engravers Hubert François Gravelot and George Michael Moser, the sculptor Louis François Roubilliac, the painters Thomas Hudson, Francis Hayman and later the young Thomas Gainsborough, the architects Isaac Ware and James Paine, the actor David Garrick, the writer Henry Fielding and Sir Martin Folkes, President of the Royal Society.

From about 1729 Hogarth obtained several commissions for 'conversation pieces' or group portraits of a family or friends, posed in a rather informal manner as if captured in their daily activities (Fig. 4). He also became increasingly interested in depicting the manners and morals of the times. Early examples of works on this theme included four paintings depicting the *Before* and *After* of seduction, in the country and in the city.[4] Hogarth then made an oil sketch showing a Harlot's *levée*, which was on display in his studio in 1730, and this seems to have been the starting point for a series of pictures showing how a prostitute had embarked on her profession and her subsequent story, entitled *A Harlot's Progress*.[5] At that period, paintings were often engraved and sold to the public by subscription, through printsellers. Hogarth, believing his series

5. *A Harlot's Progress* I, *The Arrival of the Harlot in London*, engraving

6. *A Harlot's Progress* II, *The Harlot deceiving her Jewish Protector*, engraving

7. *A Harlot's Progress* III, *The Harlot at her Dwelling in Drury Lane*, engraving

8. *A Harlot's Progress* IV, *The Harlot Beating Hemp in Bridewell*, engraving

9. *A Harlot's Progress* V, *The Death of the Harlot*, engraving

10. *A Harlot's Progress* VI, *The Funeral of the Harlot*, engraving

would have a wide appeal, decided to maximise his profits by dispensing with the printseller and taking upon himself responsibility for the engraving as well as management of the subscription. Hogarth referred to this idea as a 'still more new way of proceeding, viz painting and Engraving moder[n] moral Subject[s], a Field unbroke up in any Country or any age', perhaps an exaggerated claim as something similar but very much cruder had appeared in 17th-century Italian broadsheets. The six engravings making up *A Harlot's Progress* (Figs 5–10) were offered to subscribers and finally issued in April 1732. The cost was one guinea payable in two instalments, half on subscription and half on receipt of the prints. Hogarth seems to have made over £1,200 from the subscription which was such a great success that the series was immediately pirated by several other printsellers.

11. *The Laughing Audience*, engraving. The subscription ticket for *Southwark Fair* and *A Rake's Progress*. (© Copyright the Trustees of The British Museum)

A Harlot's Progress (the title is perhaps a deliberate and ironical reference to Bunyan's *The Pilgrim's Progress*) tells the story of Moll (or Mary) Hackabout who is seen in the first scene (Fig. 5) as an innocent country girl on her arrival in London where she falls prey to a procuress. The girl is a fictional character but the bawd would have been immediately recognisable to Hogarth's audience as Mother Needham, a notorious brothel keeper who died in May 1731 after being pilloried. Her accomplice is the man framed in the doorway: he is identifiable as Colonel Charteris, a real-life Rake convicted of rape and sent to Newgate Prison in 1730, shown fondling himself as he looks on. Such contemporary characters would have been immediately familiar to a wide audience through published broadsheets such as *Fog's Weekly Journal*. Scene II (Fig. 6) shows Moll surrounded by luxury as the kept mistress of a wealthy Jew whom she is deceiving with a clandestine lover. Her subsequent decline begins in Scene III (Fig. 7): her young and handsome lover has cost her an easy life with her keeper. She is now

12. William Hogarth, *The Marriage Contract*, c.1732–35, oil on canvas. (Ashmolean Museum, Oxford)

a common prostitute shown completing her morning *toilette* in a poorly-furnished garret in Drury Lane. The magistrate in the doorway (thought to be the Westminster magistrate Sir John Gonson, famed for harassing gamblers and prostitutes) has come to arrest her. Imprisoned in the Bridewell[6] as a common prostitute, she is shown beating hemp with other inmates in Scene IV (Fig. 8); she is then released but, ridden with syphilis, dies in poverty at the age of 23 in Scene V (Fig. 9), while her servant desperately tries to attract the attention of two doctors more interested in debating the merits of their rival prescriptions. The final scene (Fig. 10) shows her fellow prostitutes around her coffin at a gathering which is a grotesque combination of gin-induced grief and indifference. That the lesson of Moll's short life is unheeded by many of those present is shown by the two prostitutes who are taking advantage of the occasion to ply their trade, one with the undertaker (on the right) and other (to the left) with a parson who has his hand up her skirt. The vigorous depiction of ordinary life and the caricaturing of identifiable contemporaries in the *demi-monde* are aspects of Hogarth's work we shall find repeated and developed in the later series, *A Rake's Progress, Marriage A-la-Mode* and *An Election.*

The six paintings remained in Hogarth's studio until he sold them in an auction of his 'comic history-paintings' in February 1745. They were bought, along with the eight *Rake's Progress* canvases, by Alderman William Beckford, the great City merchant, for £273 (£88.4s for the *Harlot* and £184.16s for the *Rake*). Sadly, the original paintings of *A Harlot's Progress* were destroyed by fire at Beckford's Fonthill Splendens, in Wiltshire, in 1755, although it is possible that two canvases (Scenes II and IV), damaged (?by fire) and much repainted, may survive in a private collection.[7]

The success of *A Harlot's Progress* encouraged Hogarth to follow it with another series and the natural choice was the downfall of a Rake.

A RAKE'S PROGRESS

The subscription for *A Rake's Progress* opened in December 1733 and the eight prints, at a cost of 1 1/2 guineas, were promised for Michaelmas 1734. The subscription ticket depicted *The Laughing Audience* (Fig. 11).[8] Hogarth again produced a series of finished oil paintings from which the engravings were to be made. These are the eight paintings which today hang in Sir John Soane's Museum and which are described in detail on pp. 31–49.

Hogarth's painting *The Marriage Contract* in the Ashmolean Museum, Oxford, has a close connection with the *Rake* series and has generally been considered an early sketch for a somewhat different scenario (Fig. 12). When this version of the story was abandoned some details and ideas were re-used in the final version. The subject seems to be the Rake's marriage to an elderly but rich lady as in scene five of the *Rake* series (see p. 42) but much of the detail is close to *The Levée* (see p. 34), the second scene of *A Rake's Progress,* for example, the jockey with the punch-bowl.

The paintings seem to have taken Hogarth longer than he expected, for in November 1734 a notice was published saying that the prints had been delayed as he had 'found it necessary to introduce several additional characters' in the paintings.[9] He also had problems with the engraving of the plates and seems to have had some assistance in

13

14

15

16

17

18

19

20

13–20. One of the earliest of several engraved pirate versions of Hogarth's *A Rake's Progress* series, produced in June 1735 by Henry Overton, John King, Thomas Bowles and John Bowles. (© Copyright the Trustees of The British Museum)

this from Louis Scotin, a French engraver, who came to London in 1733. There was, however, another, perhaps more significant, reason for his delay in issuing the prints. Although he had profited substantially from *A Harlot's Progress*, he would have done even better if there had not been so many pirate versions. Hogarth was one of the many artists who had been pressing for the protection of their work and an Engravers' Copyright Act was at that very time before Parliament. Hogarth held up the issue of the prints until the day the Act became law on 25 June 1735.

A few pirates managed to issue their prints before 25 June but they had to work from

21. *A Rake's Progress* IV: *The Arrest, detail*

22. *A Rake's Progress* IV: *The Arrest, engraving, detail*

sketches made from memory and the oral accounts of those who had visited Hogarth's studio where the paintings were on display to prospective subscribers, rather than from Hogarth's actual prints. As a result their versions are not very close to Hogarth's own compositions. They tended to remember the main action and some particularly striking elements but the groupings and disposition of the figures often differ greatly from the originals. It is instructive to compare them with Hogarth's own prints as they show us what struck these pirates as the most memorable features of Hogarth's work. The pirate series of the *Rake* issued by Henry Overton, Thomas and John Bowles and John King is illustrated in Figs 13–20. Hogarth permitted Thomas Bakewell to issue a smaller, cheaper set of prints costing 2s 6d and these appeared in August 1735 with a broadsheet of explanatory text.

When producing engravings after paintings the design would normally be engraved on to the copper in the same direction as the painting so that when impressions were made from the plates the resulting prints would reverse the composition of the paintings. Some artists took great care to allow for this; for example in preliminary paintings and drawings they would show someone using their left hand rather than their right, which on reversal would make them right-handed. Hogarth does not always make such adjustments. In *The Arrest* (Scene IV of *A Rake's Progress*; see p. 39) the painting correctly shows White's Chocolate House on the west side of St James' Street (Fig. 21); in the engraving it is incorrectly on the east side (Fig. 22). An artist should ideally also consider the effects of reversal when working out his composition. As people are accustomed to read words from left to right, so they tend to read images in the same way, a movement from left to right seems smooth and one in the opposite direction more violent. The painting of *The Heir* (Scene I, *A Rake's Progress*; Fig. 45, p. 32) has the main action on the left and very little action on the right so that the composition seems crowded to the left. In the engraving (Fig. 47, p. 33), with the composition reversed, the left side can be considered as setting the scene and the eye moves easily with Tom's gesture towards Sarah and her mother on the right. Unusually, the engraved version of Plate II (*The Levée*; Fig. 49, p. 35) is not reversed but is the same as the painting. In the third scene (*The Orgy*; Fig. 48, p. 37) Tom is on the right in the painting and seems the most prominent figure but in the engraving, where he is on the left, he and the posture woman seem of equal importance. The fourth and fifth scenes (*The Arrest* and *The Marriage*; Figs 56 and 62, pp. 39 and 42) are others where the placing of subsidiary characters and blank space on the left in the prints make them seem rather better composed than the paintings. In the last scene (*The Madhouse*; Fig. 69, p. 47), although the Rake is placed to the left in the print (Fig. 76, p. 49), Hogarth has used lighting to emphasise him and to highlight the female visitors in the background; the rest of the scene is much more dimly lit.

The paintings themselves were made in preparation for the engravings and not as commercial items *per se*. The quality varies somewhat from painting to painting and within individual paintings, even allowing for the worn condition of the pictures. *The Marriage* (Scene V; see p. 42) is perhaps the finest, Hogarth taking great care with all the figures and their clothes and infusing the background with a cool atmospheric light (Fig. 23, detail). *The Levée* (Scene II; see p. 34) and *The Orgy* (Scene III; see p. 37) also have some very fine passages, the former being an especially good example of Hogarth's subtlety and delicacy as a colourist (Fig. 24, detail). The sinuous line formed by the heads in *The Orgy* (Fig. 25, detail) exemplifies Hogarth's use of 'the serpentine line of beauty' which he extolled in his writings. There are fine details in *The Arrest* (Scene IV, p. 39) although the street background looks rather like a stage set (Fig. 26, detail). The glow of light on the faces of the figures on the extreme right of *The Gaming House* (Scene VI, p. 44) is masterly (Fig. 27, detail) but the painting is uneven. However, the lack of smooth finish in these paintings appeals greatly to the modern eye and looks forward to the freely painted works of Hogarth's late period such as *The Shrimp Girl* and *The Staymaker*.

Hogarth had considerable influence on British and even European art, and portraits painted in the 1740s and 1750s by Joshua Reynolds, Thomas Gainsborough and Allan Ramsay, before the Grand Style became general, reflect the naturalness and realism of his portraits. The literary and theatrical quality of his works also inspired paintings depicting scenes from Shakespeare and contemporary novels or recording stage performances. Joseph Highmore painted twelve scenes from Samuel Richardson's *Pamela*, a popular novel published in 1740, which are charming but much simpler than Hogarth's series with only a few characters in each scene and without the wealth of detail commenting on and adding depth to the story. Later caricaturists and satirists such as James Gillray and Thomas Rowlandson also owe much to Hogarth's example.

23. *A Rake's Progress* V: *The Marriage*, detail

Hogarth's engravings circulated on the Continent and had considerable influence there. The engraver, Hubert Gravelot, having done much to introduce the Rococo to England when he moved here from France in 1732, on his return to France in 1745 helped to spread the influence of Hogarth's moral realism in the other direction. European artists who were influenced, to a greater or lesser degree, by Hogarth include J B Greuze, Pietro Longhi, Francisco Goya and Honoré Daumier. Hogarth's treatise on painting, *The Analysis of Beauty*, 1753, was more influential on the Continent than in Britain and the writers and critics who alluded to it and to his paintings included the Frenchman Diderot and the Germans Charles L Hagedorn, Georg Christoph Lichtenberg and Gottold Ephraim Lessing.

We know a good deal about Hogarth's intentions in his engravings and the way his contemporaries interpreted them from texts and descriptions written at the time or soon after. Hogarth's friend Dr John Hoadly (1711–76) wrote a moralising verse to accompany each plate of *A Rake's Progress*. The smaller copies which Hogarth authorised Thomas Bakewell to issue had a different set of verses and a broadsheet to accompany them: *An Explanation of the Eight Prints of the Rake's Progress*. Most of the pirate editions

24. *A Rake's Progress*, II: *The Levée*, detail

25. *A Rake's Progress* III: *The Orgy*, detail

26. *A Rake's Progress* IV: *The Arrest*, detail

27. *A Rake's Progress* VI: *The Gaming House*, detail

also had verses of comment. Other poems appeared separately such as *The Rake's Progress; or, the Humours of Drury Lane. A Poem. In Eight Canto's*, London, 1735. Continental buyers were not ignored, for Hogarth commissioned Jean André Rouquet, a French-Swiss engraver resident in London, to write a description of his engravings in French – *Lettres de Monsieur ** à un de ses Amis a Paris, pour lui expliquer les Estampes de Monsieur Hogarth*, London, 1746.

The anecdotal character of Hogarth's paintings had a considerable influence on contemporary writers. These include Samuel Richardson, the author of *Pamela* and *Clarissa* and also of *Familiar Letters* in which one letter describes Bedlam as housing a man crossed in love and the casual amusement with which visitors, especially females, regarded the inmates. Henry Fielding, the author of *Joseph Andrews*, *Tom Jones*, *Amelia* and *Jonathan Wild* makes several allusions to Hogarth's works in his writings and probably took certain incidents from him. For example, in both *Jonathan Wild* and *Amelia* a woman swoons on visiting her loved one in prison. Tobias Smollett, who wrote *Roderick Random* and *Peregrine Pickle*, includes in the latter a nobleman being arrested for debt as he steps into his chair at the door of White's Chocolate House. All of these show knowledge of *A Rake's Progress*.

In the 20th century Hogarth's *A Rake's Progress* has been used as the basis for both a ballet and an opera. The first performance of Ninette de Valois's ballet *A Rake's Progress* was given in 1935 by the Sadler's Wells Ballet with Walter Gore as the Rake and Alicia Markova as the Betrayed Girl. The music was by Gavin Gordon and the designs by Rex Whistler, after Hogarth. The ballet followed the story as depicted by Hogarth very closely. It is still revived at intervals by the Royal Ballet. Igor Stravinsky's opera *The Rake's Progress* (produced in Venice in 1951) on the other hand, has a libretto by W H Auden and Chester Kallman which is only remotely connected with Hogarth's series in that the Rake is called Tom Rakewell and it has scenes set in a brothel and a madhouse. Otherwise its story is quite different and in many ways much more akin to that of Faust. In this country the opera has been produced at Sadler's Wells and Covent Garden but perhaps the most famous production was that staged at Glyndebourne in 1975, which was designed by David Hockney, who also produced a series of etchings inspired by *A Rake's Progress*.

Returning to the paintings themselves, Hogarth kept *A Rake's Progress* in his own possession until 1745, when it was sold at auction to William Beckford the Elder, along with *A Harlot's Progress*, for 84 guineas and hung at Fonthill Splendens, his house in Wiltshire. In 1787, at the beginning of his career as an architect, John Soane was commissioned by Beckford's son, William Beckford the Younger, to design a gallery at Fonthill (which was not in the end built). Soane visited Fonthill on 25 April and 3 December 1787 and would have seen Beckford's fine collection.[10] On 27 February 1802 much of William Beckford's collection was sold at Christie's and Mrs Soane bought *A Rake's Progress* for 570 guineas (Soane was only just recovering from illness and she was bidding on his behalf).

During the seven or eight years following the completion of *A Rake's Progress* Hogarth was chiefly engaged in painting large-scale (life-size) portraits, such as *The Graham Children* (National Gallery, London) and *Captain Coram* (The Foundling Hospital Museum, London). It was not until 1743 that Hogarth announced his next 'modern moral subject'.

MARRIAGE A-LA-MODE

Hogarth decided to produce another series of paintings dealing with contemporary manners and morals but this time following the fortunes and charting the downfall of two characters of higher rank than in his earlier Progresses. Hogarth saw these paintings (see Figs 28 and 35) not just as preparations for the engravings but also as works of art in their own right though he was disappointed in the price they eventually fetched when they were sold in June 1751. He had to bring them to a highly finished state, as he had decided not to engrave them himself but instead to employ two French engravers to produce the plates, although he promised to engrave 'the Heads' himself 'for the better Preservation of the Characters and Expressions'. Hogarth hoped the prints might appeal to a wider market and his advertisement of April 1743 declared they

28. *Marriage-A-la-Mode* II, *The Tête à Tête*, oil on canvas. (© The National Gallery, London)

29. *Marriage A-la-Mode*, I, *The Marriage Settlement*, etching and engraving

30. *Marriage A-la-Mode*, II, *The Tête à Tête*, etching and engraving

31. *Marriage A-la-Mode*, III, *The Inspection*, etching and engraving

would depict 'a Variety of Modern Occurences in High-Life, and [would be] called Marriage A-la-Mode. Particular Care will be taken, that there may not be the least Objection to the Decency or Elegancy of the whole Work, and that none of the Characters represented shall be personal.'[11]

The six engravings of *Marriage A-la-Mode* were published in April–May 1745 (Figs 29 to 34).[12] The 'High Life' elements in the series reflect Hogarth's observation that those with money often have what he himself called 'bad taste', slavishly following fashions in dress and manners, preferring 'Masquerades and Operas' to good English plays and pretending to connoisseurship by buying copies of old masters instead of using their own judgement to acquire works by living British artists. He had already lampooned such characters in *Taste in High Life*, painted in 1742 (sometimes called *Taste à la Mode*). The French style of the engraving associates the series with engravings after *fêtes gallantes* by Watteau and Hogarth's dislike of foreign (and particularly French) airs and graces is implicit in many of the scenes.

As Judy Egerton has observed, *Marriage A-la-Mode* is a melodrama, both comic and serious, tracing how a marriage was made and wrecked.[13] The series begins (Fig. 29) with a marriage arranged by two ambitious fathers – an old nobleman, Earl Squander, and a wealthy but plebeian Alderman of the City of London. This scene has its model in conversation pictures of the kind Hogarth had specialised in during the 1730s and is set in the Earl's Chamber, the accustomed place for the signing of a marriage contract (see Fig. 12, p. 15). The title of the series makes it clear that the marriage is one of convenience and it is the moneyed Alderman who holds centre stage, with the bride and groom to the left and the nobleman on the right. In this marriage, in effect, the parents are selling their children. The nobleman's son, Viscount Squanderfield, will succeed to the title Earl Squander, financially secure through the wealth of his new wife, who will gain social status by becoming Lady Squander and a Countess. The subsequent five scenes chart the progress of this marriage which begins with money and ends with adultery, venereal disease, murder and suicide. In the second scene the Viscount is shown collapsed in a chair, having returned from a night on the town, and ignoring his wife. A lady's bonnet protruding from his pocket (his wife is wearing <u>her</u> bonnet) hints at infidelity. The beauty patch on his neck almost certainly covers a syphilitic sore – this Squanderfield 'squanders' his passion on prostitutes. In the next scene the Viscount, accompanied by a very young girl, is in a Doctor's consulting room. He seems to be the patient and to be complaining that the doctor's pills – probably black mercurial pills for venereal disease – don't work. The child holds a pill box, perhaps indicating that she – through the Viscount – has also been infected. The furious woman may be the procuress who has provided the young girl.[14] The final three scenes depict the tragic end to the story. In *The Toilette* (Fig. 32) the new Countess Squander (note the Earl's coronet on the bed) is holding court, with the lawyer, Silvertongue, seen talking with her in Scene I, a welcome guest with his feet up on the sofa. Scene V, *The Bagnio*, is set at night in one of the London coffee houses which were also equipped with Turkish baths. Many such places chiefly provided rooms for the night with no questions asked. The Countess and Silvertongue have met there after attending a masquerade, but their plans for an illicit night together have backfired. The Count has burst into the room and been fatally wounded by Silvertongue, who flees through the window. In the final scene, the wretched Countess, with at her feet a report of Silvertongue's final speech from the Gallows, commits

32. *Marriage A-la-Mode*, IV, *The Toilette*, etching and engraving

33. *Marriage A-la-Mode*, V, *The Bagnio*, etching and engraving

35. *Marriage A-la-Mode*, VI, *The Lady's Death*, oil on canvas. (© The National Gallery, London)

34. *Marriage A-la-Mode*, VI, *The Lady's Death*, etching and engraving

suicide. Her child, the sole heir in whom rank and wealth were intended to combine for the worldly advancement of the two families, is left an orphan, condemned to death by congenital syphilis. The Alderman, in a final act of greed, prevents his daughter returning her child's last embrace by grabbing her arm in order to remove a ring from her finger (a suicide's chattels were forfeit).

Hogarth planned a companion series to *Marriage A-la-Mode* entitled *The Happy Marriage*, for which at least two sketches survive (*The Staymaker* (?*The Happy Marriage* V: *The Fitting of the Ball Gown*) and *The Dance* (*The Happy Marriage* ?VI: *The Country Dance; Fig. 36*), both in the Tate. His intention in this six-part series was to contrast the immoral life in London depicted in *Marriage A-la-Mode* with a series of scenes depicting the old-fashioned virtues of country life. The series was never completed.

In 1751 Hogarth offered the paintings of *Marriage A-la-Mode* for sale 'to the Highest Bidder', by a system of written bids. He considered them among the best things he had ever painted with their finely observed detail, high level of finish and subtle colouring. The result of the sale, to John Lane, who was one of only two bidders, was a bitter disappointment as the series fetched only £126. John Lane retained the paintings until his death in 1791 – refusing all offers for them. His heir, one Colonel Cawthorne MP, offered them for sale at Christie's on 10 March 1792, but they failed to sell. He then mortgaged them to a Mr Holmes, on whose behalf they were finally sold by Christie's on 10 February 1797 for 1,000 guineas to John Julius Angerstein. Angerstein was a great admirer of Hogarth. Following his death in 1823, the pictures were purchased with the Angerstein collection for the nation. When the new National Gallery opened its doors in Pall Mall in May 1824, *Marriage A-la-Mode* was on display and the series remains in the National Gallery today (see Figs 28 and 35).

36. William Hogarth, *The Happy Marriage ?VI, The Country Dance*, 1754, oil on canvas.
(© Tate, London 2007)

Hogarth's inspiration for his final 'modern moral subject' series, *An Election,* was the notorious contest for the town and country parliamentary seats in Oxfordshire during the General Election of 1754. During this period the manipulation of the electorate through propaganda and bribery was commonplace. New heights of political sleaze were reached in the Oxfordshire election, however, and the campaign became notorious, receiving wide coverage in contemporary journals and pamphlets. In the words of *The London Evening Post,* 'Every British Heart is full of the Oxfordshire Election, which is become the chief subject of Conversation in the remotest corners of the Island.'[15] In the eighteenth century, as today, mounting an election campaign could be hugely expensive, particularly as at this time the process involved mobilising votes through bribery. It was usual, therefore, for seats to go uncontested in order to save money.

Since the accession of the Hanoverians to the throne in 1714, the Tories had been eclipsed in power by the Whig party who cast them, often unfairly, as Jacobites (i.e. traitors loyal to the interests of the exiled Catholic Stuarts, first the deposed King James II and later his son James Stuart, the 'Old Pretender', and grandson, Charles Edward Stuart – 'Bonnie Prince Charlie'). This was accompanied by the much more severe accusation of 'Popery' which one propagandist described as 'a millstone . . . about the neck of old interest'. While the Whigs, the Party of the New Interest, included some very powerful landowners they also had links with the City and the growing mercantile classes and had some sympathy for the Protestant Dissenters. They were the party of power and had held a large majority in Parliament since the 1715 election held soon after the accession of George I, but had split into factions who competed to monopolise Ministerial Office and the administration of the country. The faction in power at any one time was regarded as the Court Party, and unsuccessful factions would join with the Tories to form the Opposition or Country Party. In Hogarth's *Election* paintings their usual green colour is replaced by orange.

In 1754 the Tory candidates for Oxfordshire were Sir James Dashwood and Lord Wenman of Thame and Caswell. To the opposing Whigs the Jacobitism of the former was demonstrated not only by the Jacobite sympathies of many of his friends but by the fact that he had planted Scottish firs on his country estate at Kirtlington Park. The main impetus for a challenge to the Tories in Oxfordshire came from Charles Spencer, 3rd Duke of Marlborough, a Whig who nurtured ambitions to be an important political patron. It was Marlborough's support that helped launch the campaign in Oxfordshire, which began in earnest in 1752, two years before the election itself. The Whig candidates were Sir Edward Turner (an ambitious local landowner who had been expelled from the Commons in 1747 for shady practices at his election for Great Bedwyn) and Lord Parker (Thomas Parker), son of the powerful Earl of Macclesfield.

All male forty-shilling freeholders were entitled to vote (an electorate in Oxfordshire of about 4,000), although even the assessment of eligibility was open to manipulation by the political parties. The Oxfordshire campaigns of both parties were not confined to speech-making and pamphleteering but included the provision of 'treats' for prospective electors which, for the more affluent and influential, might take the form of gifts of wine or venison, and for the less important, dinners and entertainments at

37. *Crowns, Mitres, Maces etc.*, engraved subscription ticket for *An Election*. (© Copyright the Trustees of The British Museum)

38. *An Election* I, detail

which much food was provided and alcohol flowed in torrents. Oliver Goldsmith, in *Citizen of the World*, said of elections that 'the merits of a candidate are often measured by the number of his treats; his constituents assemble, eat upon him, and lend their applause not to his integrity of sense but the quantities of his beef and brandy.' Even the ladies were not forgotten for although they could not vote, they might well be able to influence their male relatives. So gifts were distributed such as gloves and lace. Important local craftsmen, businessmen and shopkeepers suddenly found themselves being patronised by local magnates. Processions were held and banners were carried attacking the policy of the opposing party and emphasising the patriotism and respect for liberty of the Party organising the procession. This often provoked opposition from supporters of the other Party and fighting, often involving bands of hired thugs, would ensue.

The *Election* series is part of a long tradition of political satire on the theme of the vices attendant on rural election campaigns. In 1741 a poem, *The Humours of a Country Election*, was published in London and may have had some influence on Hogarth's series as its frontispiece included illustrations of a scene outside an inn and of the chairing of the successful candidates by an unruly mob as well as an account of how the writer was invited by the 'Drawer at the Inn' [the tapster] to attend a treat. Hogarth himself had begun to take up political themes with his print *Country Inn Yard at Election Time* of 1747.

In March 1754, Hogarth began issuing the print *Crowns Mitres, Maces etc* (Fig. 37), as a receipt to subscribers to his *Four Prints of an Election*. Although the first painting, *An Election Entertainment*, was put on display just days before the May election, it seems likely that he was still working on the remainder of the paintings for much of 1754–55 as the last painting, *Chairing the Member*, has the date 1755 on the sundial. The engravings were delayed and the last two plates at least, were not finished until January 1758 (Plate IV, Figs 97–98, p. 63) and February 1758 (Plate III, Figs 91–92, pp. 59–60). Although the paintings and engravings were inspired by the 1754 election and especially the events in Oxfordshire, the backgrounds are generic and, while the series includes several portraits, they are not those of the main protagonists. Hogarth has distilled what interested him most from what he read, and the series becomes perhaps his most bitter comment on human folly. He does not seem to have felt that the mere fact that, for the first time since 1710, electors were being given a chance to exercise their rights and duties as citizens was in any way an advance to be applauded.

An Election, in contrast to *A Rake's Progress*, is very finely painted and the series ranks as one of Hogarth's greatest masterpieces. There is no variation in quality from painting to painting or within any one painting; each detail is lovingly finished, however repulsive the subject, and the paint is freely and richly applied. Hogarth's palette seems to have become more varied and better balanced.

The paintings are much larger than those of *A Rake's Progress* (101.5 × 127 cm compared with 62.2 × 75 cm) and the compositions are more complex and carefully worked out. His keen observation of mankind is shown in the superb series of heads; it is true they are nearly all slightly caricatured but they are all so real that one can speculate about their life outside the paintings. The interior setting of the first scene is far more solidly constructed and more naturally lit than any interior in the *Rake* except perhaps the church which is the setting for *The Marriage* (Scene V). The landscapes and townscapes of the other three pictures seem to encompass the action rather than being just

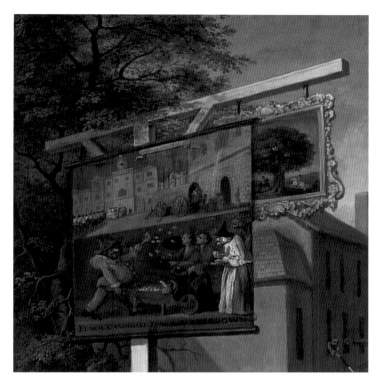

39. *An Election* II, detail

41. *An Election* IV, detail

40. *An Election* II, detail

42. *An Election* IV, detail

a backdrop. The background landscapes in *An Election* II and III are very finely painted (see Fig. 40) and the lighting unifies them into a whole with the foreground. The quality of the paintwork, the golden light suffusing the landscapes and the richer, brighter palette almost disguise the fact that the subject is a study of the cupidity, corruption and folly of mankind unrelieved by any figure of innocence, such as Sarah Young in the *Rake*, or by any suggestion of the protagonists being the unfortunate victims of the machinations of others, as in *Marriage A-la-Mode*. This pessimistic view of humanity as a mass of drunken, greedy, and stupid individuals may well reflect Hogarth's unhappiness towards the end of his life when he found that many of his ideals both for art and for everyday life were being superseded.

The four engravings of *An Election* had no accompanying verses but Hogarth authorised the publication of *A Poetical Description of Mr Hogarth's Election Prints, in four Cantos. Written under Mr Hogarth's Sanction and Inspection*, London, 1759.

In 1761 Hogarth included Scene I of *An Election, An Election Entertainment* in the group of works he exhibited at the Society of Artists' exhibition in Spring Gardens: with seven canvases on show he was the chief contributor. The inclusion of *An Election Entertainment* signalled his increasing interest in political as opposed to social satire.

Hogarth's *An Election* series was bought from the artist by his close friend David Garrick, the famous actor, in 1762 (Fig. 43).[16] According to Mrs Garrick's later reminiscences, Hogarth could not find a purchaser for the series so decided to sell it by subscription and Garrick went to look at the paintings. He liked them and agreed to subscribe but, as he was leaving, he suddenly thought that he could easily afford to buy them and would thus save his friend Hogarth any further disgrace or trouble. He went back and paid the full amount Hogarth wanted – £200. Mrs Garrick said she believed her husband never laid out his money to better advantage.[17] Soane would have seen *An Election* in 1814 when Mrs Garrick lent the four paintings to the British Institution's exhibition of *Pictures by the late William Hogarth, Richard Wilson, Thomas Gainsborough and J. Zoffani*; he himself lent *A Rake's Progress*. Garrick died in 1779 but his widow lived on until October 1822. On 23 June 1823 her effects were sold at Christie's and Soane bought *An Election* for 1650 guineas. John Britton, in *The Union of Architecture, Sculpture and Painting*, 1827, the first published guidebook to Soane's collections, wrote of *An Election*:

> 'The four pictures . . . may be referred to as the best essay ever published on *Parliamentary Reform*. Here bribery and corruption, with their consequences, drunkenness, gluttony, cruelty, and human debasement, are shown in hideous colours, and with hideous expressions. Such a set of pictures should occupy a separate vestibule to the English House of Commons; to show errors and vices that are tolerated and even promoted by members of that assembly, but which reflect disgrace on themselves and impeach the good sense of the country. Every true patriot and honest man would thus be perpetually reminded of the absolute necessity of modifying or abolishing the present system of elections. Though these pictures are not so well known as others of Hogarth's, they may be regarded as the most complete, comprehensive, and perhaps, his best, as a series. We are aware that the 'Marriage-à-la-Mode' is the most popular, and that they abound with merit, both as works of art and as embracing a fine moral

43. William Hogarth, David Garrick and his wife, Eva-Maria Veigel, 1757, oil on canvas. (The Royal Collection © 2007, Her Majesty Queen Elizabeth II)

essay; but the Election pictures are larger . . . more diversified in matter and subject, contain more of incident, character and graphic display . . . From the commencement of canvassing, through the various stages of bribery, cajoling, intriguery, and deception, up to conquest and riotous exultation, on the one part; with the usual accompaniment of vindictive and rancorous opposition, ending in fighting and other acts of barbarous hostility, on the other. As indicative of the vulgarity and bestiality of contested elections, the painter has introduced pigs, monkeys, chimney-sweeps, and the very lowest classes of society, in juxtaposition with nobles of the land . . .'

HOGARTH'S FINAL YEARS

Hogarth continued to paint and to produce engravings until his death in 1764 but the pessimistic view of humanity which is found in *An Election* reflects his growing disillusionment with the world around him. The younger generation of artists looked increasingly to the Old Masters for inspiration and his own attempt to prove that a British artist could equal Correggio (*Sigismunda Mourning over the Heart of Guiscardo*, 1759; Fig. 44) was rejected by the man who had commissioned it and widely ridiculed.[18] He did not support the growing demand for the founding of a National Academy as he felt it might be too rigid and autocratic but in this he was out of step with most of his fellow artists. He was also criticised by John Wilkes for entering into 'the poor politics of the faction of the day' and his work attracted increasingly polarised responses. He suffered from ill health in his last years but still managed to produce the engraving entitled *The Times, Plate I* (1762) attacking those who were hostile to peace because they were profiting from the war. By the time of Hogarth's death he was both the most celebrated and the most vilified artist in Britain. His final engraving *The Bathos* (1764), issued only a few months before his death, is one of his darkest works, a totally pessimistic image of the condition of the Arts in England and of the state of the country itself.

Within two years of Hogarth's death the first book devoted to his work began to appear in parts, the Revd John Trusler's *Hogarth Moralized*. Trusler also wrote a farce inspired by *An Election* called *The Country Election*, in 1768. Other early works on Hogarth are listed in the Bibliography including the important *Biographical Anecdotes* of John Nichols, George Steevens, Isaac Reed etc. and John Ireland's *Hogarth Illustrated*.

Soane's Hogarths are some of the painter's most important works and are rightly considered among the Museum's greatest treasures. Even in periods when Hogarth was not as highly regarded as he is today these paintings were admired for their narrative quality and for the imaginative yet realistic depiction of the manners and morals of 18th-century England. Today, when Hogarth is one of the most highly regarded of English artists, we also appreciate the beauty of his paintwork and his ability to make each of the actors in his dramas a three-dimensional human being.

44. William Hogarth, *Sigismunda Mourning over the Heart of Guiscardo*, 1759, oil on canvas (© Tate, London 2007)

Description of the eight paintings and the engravings of A Rake's Progress

SCENE I: THE HEIR

The first scene (Fig. 45) introduces the two main actors in the drama, Tom Rakewell and Sarah Young and tells us much about the background of the former. Hogarth's Rake is no scion of the aristocracy but the son and heir of a miserly moneylender. We are shown a room in the father's house, not long after his death. The details of this first scene reveal how he made his wealth, 'raking it in' and hoarding it, spending as little as possible, and the whole series goes on to show how his heir, the Rake, proceeds to spend it all in seeking to establish himself in Society.

The ceiling and walls of the room are cracked, there is no carpet on the floor, the chimney-piece is plain, and the heavy chair and diamond-paned window are old-fashioned. A portrait of the father is hung over the mantelpiece showing him weighing and counting (i.e. 'raking in') his gold. It is certainly a portrait and not a genre painting as a cap identical to that worn by the protagonist hangs on the mantelshelf directly beneath it. The clean and empty fireplace shows that he has not wasted money on heating but has kept himself warm with this cap and the heavy coat hanging on the door.

In the centre foreground is a chest filled with silver and money bags labelled '1000', '2000' and '3000'. An emaciated cat is peering into it hoping to find something to eat. Beside the chest is a pile of papers some of which are inscribed 'Mortgages' 'India Bonds' and 'Funds'. In the lower right-hand corner is the father's journal on which is written 'Memo[ran]^{dums} 1720 / May 3^d My Son Tom / came from Oxford / 4th Din[e]^d at the / French Ordinary / 5th of June - Put of[f] / my bad Shilling.' Despite all his wealth, he could not bear the prospect of the loss of a single shilling and considers his success in dishonestly passing a counterfeit one on to someone else a matter worth recording in his journal! Samuel Johnson in his *Dictionary* defined an 'Ordinary', in this context, as 'A Place of eating established at a certain price'. As a man nails up black mourning hangings the rotten cornice of the room crumbles to reveal more gold coins hidden behind it. An escutcheon very appropriate to the deceased has been placed on the hangings: three vices screwed tight with the motto 'Beware'. On the mantelpiece is a 'save-all': a small pan inserted into a candlestick to save the ends of the candles.

Cupboards and boxes have been thrown open so that an inventory can be made of the dead man's goods, although these, apart from the hoarded wealth, are likely to prove almost worthless as it seems he always tried to avoid buying anything new and never threw anything away. A pair of spectacles without lenses hangs on the chimney-piece and a cupboard is stuffed with old shoes, boots and wigs, two swords, a bowl and a broken jug. In the bottom right-hand corner, above the journal, is a box with a spade and a broken lantern.

45. *A Rake's Progress* I: *The Heir*

The Heir, Tom, is depicted as a fresh-faced and reasonably attractive youth although his expression suggests a lack of intelligence and feeling; a superficial character easily led and duped. In contrast to his father's avarice and careful hoarding of every penny Tom Rakewell has no hesitation in spending his inheritance freely, indeed squandering it on every luxury and comfort which his father denied himself. Putting up black hangings around the room is a mark of respect for the deceased but one that his father would probably have considered a useless extravagance. On a roll of the material on the chair on the left is a bill from the supplier, 'London / Bought of / Wm. Tothall / Woollen Drap/er in Covent / Garden'. William Tothall was a close friend of Hogarth and one of his companions in his 'Peregrination' into Kent in May 1732.

The figure seated at the table is making an inventory of Tom's inheritance. The father would never have entrusted this job to anyone but himself and indeed while Tom's back is turned, the man, with a sly expression on his face, is stealing from a bag of gold. The man has been variously identified as a steward, an undertaker, or a lawyer. The Bakewell broadsheet, which accompanied Thomas Bakewell's authorised engravings after *A Rake's Progress*, says he is a 'Lawyer, by his dress . . . employ'd to make an inventory of the Estate'. Hogarth probably disliked lawyers as a result of his own involvement in a law suit some years before.

On the extreme left is the other main protagonist of the series, Sarah Young, a girl whom Tom has seduced at Oxford and whom he is trying to pay off now that he is rich and about to enter Society. There seems little doubt that he previously promised to marry her for she holds a wedding ring in her hand and on the letters spilling out of her mother's apron can be deciphered the phrases 'To Mrs. Sarah Young in Oxford . . .' and 'Dearest Life . . . & marry you'. Sarah wears a pink rose tucked in her dress, matching the pink ribbons of her cap: no doubt she had set out with her mother in expectation of being greeted with delight by her lover. Now that he rejects her and denies his promises and the ring he gave her, she turns away weeping and, if left to herself, ready to withdraw in hurt silence. However, her mother is not so easily thwarted and she makes a threatening gesture, drawing attention to Sarah's pregnant state. Tom's face shows no feeling of sympathy, regret or any trace of guilt. The handful of money which he is offering seems pitifully little.

Hogarth produced several versions (or states) of the engraving he made after this painting, re-working the copperplate each time to make the desired alterations. The first and second states of the engraving are very close to the painting (allowing for the usual reversal) except that the old woman in the background is laying the fire with faggots rather than wood shavings (Fig. 46). The papers around the chest in the foreground have been rearranged and more inscriptions are visible including 'Lease & Release', 'Fines & Recoverys' and 'This . . . Indenture'. The journal is dated 1721 not 1720 and the lay-out of the text is slightly different. In the third state Hogarth made several alterations. Sarah's face is completely changed and is partly hidden by her handkerchief (Fig. 47). Tothall's bill has been removed and the journal now lies on the right with only one page visible; 'May 1st' replaces 'May 3^{d}', and the lay-out of the text is again changed. Its place on the left is taken by a large family Bible from the cover of which the father has removed a piece of leather to resole his shoes.

46. *A Rake's Progress* I, engraving, second state. (The Royal Collection © 2007, Her Majesty Queen Elizabeth II)

47. *A Rake's Progress* I, engraving, third state

SCENE II: THE LEVÉE

Tom is using his inheritance to buy his way into London Society and he is shown at his morning *levée* (a morning audience with visitors and tradespeople; adopted by fashionable British aristocrats from French court culture which Hogarth probably despised) surrounded by hangers-on seeking the patronage of such a liberal spender (Fig. 48). The surroundings are more spacious than the humble room of the first scene and no ordinary domestic utensils are visible. Large, fashionable, windows light the room and the pictures have richly ornamented and gilded frames very different from the plain frame of the portrait in the first scene. The subject of the central painting, *The Judgement of Paris*, with its mythological subject the choice, by Paris, of the most beautiful woman in the world which led to the abduction of Helen, the Trojan war and his own downfall,

48. A Rake's Progress II: *The Levée*

highlights Tom's own dubious moral choices, which will lead to his downfall. Paris's choice of Venus is juxtaposed with Tom's preference for a dubious body-guard. The painting is obviously by one of the foreign old masters whose favoured position with the fashionable man of taste was so much resented by Hogarth who wrote elsewhere: 'The connoisseurs and I are at war you know; and because I hate them they think I hate Titian and let them.'[19] He was as much a critic of the taste of the period as of its vices, and here he shows Tom's lack of artistic judgement. This is emphasised by the contrast with the flanking pictures of fighting-cocks which hardly seem fitting in such a grand room. These, combined with the presence of a jockey (front, right) presenting him with a silver punchbowl, won by his horse at Newmarket, show his taste for sport and, perhaps, a penchant for gambling. The punchbowl is engraved with a portrait of a race horse and the words 'Won at Newmarket' and 'Silly Tom' (the eponymous name of his horse) along with the date of victory, 'Sep[r] 10 1727', showing several years have passed since the first scene. Behind the jockey is a huntsman, blowing his horn.

Tom has not yet dressed and he is seen wearing a fashionable dressing gown and slippers; as he has not yet put on his wig his shaven head is covered with a cap. He is turning to a man who has just handed him a letter of introduction on which can be read 'Sr. Capt Hackum is / a man of Honor his / support may serve yo[u] / I am Sir / your most obed[ient] / Hum[bl][e] Ser[van][t] / W Stab.' This thickset ruffian is brandishing his sword with one hand and placing his other hand on his heart as if swearing his honesty and allegiance. He is offering to act for Tom in any necessity. Tom's fencing master is shown on the left making a pass with his foil; notice the button on the point. He is a portrait of Dubois, a well-known French master who was killed in a duel in 1733. Behind him, regarding him rather disapprovingly, is James Figg (d.1734), a prize-fighter at whose 'amphitheatre' at the sign of the City of Oxford, in Oxford Road, fashionable young men could learn some of the natural arts of defence – he is holding a quarter-staff (wooden stave).

On the extreme left is a musician seated at a harpsichord and playing music inscribed 'The Rape of the Sabines, an Opera by F.H.'; the list of performers on the second page is not legible. 'F.H.' must be a reference to George Frederick Handel, one of the leading composers of the time and a protégé of Lord Burlington whose taste in art Hogarth had satirised. Although he was a naturalised British subject, Hogarth would have seen Handel as the composer of operas in Italian not English; operas in which the leading parts were usually taken by Italian singers, many of them *castrati*. As the musician is only seen from behind, we cannot tell if it is Handel himself who has graced Tom's *levée*. Another musician, a French-horn player, appears on the extreme right.

Almost centre front is a very stylish, even affected, dancing master holding the small fiddle or 'kit' with which he will accompany his pupil during the lesson. Early commentators assume that he is a Parisian, another foreigner. The landscape gardener behind him is thought to be a portrait of Charles Bridgeman (d.1738), who was primarily responsible for the change in fashion from formal to picturesque landscape gardening, although the plan he holds, marked 'Plan 2', shows little imagination. The figures in the ante-room in the left background include a tailor, a milliner and a poet who has written a piece in honour of Tom.

The first two paintings of *A Rake's Progress* form a contrasting pair; the first detailing all the petty and mean acts of niggardliness of an old miser and the second all the excesses of a young spendthrift.

The engraved version of *The Levée* is not reversed and Hogarth employed Louis Scotin to finish the engraving. The first (proof) state (Fig. 49) is close to the painting but many of the faces are only lightly etched and the writing has not yet been put on the cup, the score and the letter in Tom's hand. The second (proof) state (Fig. 50), shows more work on the faces, except that of James Figg which is completely blank. A long scroll now hangs over the harpsichordist's chair but it is blank, as are all the other pieces of paper and inscribed surfaces. In the later (third and fourth states; see Fig. 51), various inscriptions have been amended or added. The cup is engraved 'Won at Epsom' (not Newmarket) and 'Silly Tom' but there is no date. The letter in Tom's hand reads 'S[r] the Capt[ain] / is a Man of / Honour, his / Sword may serve / you /yr[s] W[m] Stab.' A short

49. *A Rake's Progress* II, engraving, first state. (The Royal Collection © 2007, Her Majesty Queen Elizabeth II)

50. *A Rake's Progress* II, engraving, second state. (The Royal Collection © 2007, Her Majesty Queen Elizabeth II)

51. *A Rake's Progress* II, engraving, third state

inscription 'Epistle / to / Rakew[ell] . . .' can be read on the paper in the hand of the poet by the window. On the score is written 'The / Rape of / the Sabines / a New / Opera' and a list of 'Performers':

Romulus	Sen: [Signor] Fari[nel]li
Ravisher	Sen: Sen[esi]no
2 [i.e. second] Ravisher	Sen: Car[estri]ne
3 Ravisher	Sen: Coz – n [Signora Cuzzoni]
Sabine Women	Sen^ra Str - - dr [Strada]
	Sen^ra Ber[tol]le'

On the scroll hanging over the chair is written:

'List of the Rich Presents Signor Farinelli the Italian Singer Condescended to Accept of Y^e English Nobility & Gentry for One Night's Performance in the Opera Artaserses [*Artaserse* or Artaxerxes] – A pair of Diamond Knee Buckles Presented by—A Diamond Ring by—A Bank Note enclosed in a Rich Gold Case by—A Gold Snuff box Chac'd [sic = chased] with the story of Orpheus Charming y^e Brutes [presented] by T. Rakewell Esq. 100 . . . 20 . . . 100.'

An engraving on the floor at the end of the scroll shows Farinelli enthroned with an altar before him and a host of admiring ladies offering him their hearts and crying, 'One God One Farinelli'. This is the illustration to 'A Poem Dedicated to T. Rakewell Esq.'. All the singers named actually existed, Farinelli, Senesino and Carestrine being *castrati* and therefore somewhat inappropriately cast as ravishers; 'Coz-n', playing the third ravisher, refers to Signora Cuzzoni, again perhaps not quite what one would expect but the various female singers portraying Sabine women or virgins (Strada, Negri and Bertolle) were not noted for the rectitude of their private lives. Such jokes can only be appreciated in the engravings: in the painting such details would have been too laborious to add, requiring a painstaking technique at odds with the lively broad-brush technique Hogarth uses. Farinelli made his London debut on 29 October 1734 in J A Hasse's *Artaxerxes* and was showered with gifts. The rapturous cry, 'One God One Farinelli', is reported to have been made by Lady Rich, a lover of opera, to express her feelings on hearing him singing. Hogarth must have hastened to add this latest example of human folly to the engravings on which he was working even though it meant quite considerable alteration to the plate. The harpsichord is labelled 'J Mahoon Fecit'; Joseph Mahoon was an important London harpsichord-maker who supplied instruments to the Crown.

SCENE III: THE ORGY

Tom Rakewell spends his evenings and nights in even more riotous living and is seen here visiting the notorious Rose Tavern, Covent Garden (Fig. 52). The broken lantern and staff beside his chair suggest that on his way to the tavern he has indulged in a favourite sport of the young men of the town, attacking the Watch and seizing their insignia as trophies. Tom sprawls on the right with his clothes in disarray and a foolish expression on his face.[20] He is already very drunk and does not notice that his female companion, who is fondling him, has stolen his watch and is passing it

52. *A Rake's Progress* III: *The Orgy*

to her accomplice. The watch shows that the time is three o'clock in the morning.

One of the girls entertains another client, who seems to be a Chinese tradesman, in the background. Her cap and dress are in some disorder and his wig is falling off to reveal his close-cropped hair underneath. In the absence of clients the other ladies of the town have to amuse themselves. The two on the left are drinking; one is swilling down punch so avidly that it spills over the edge of the bowl, and the other aping a more refined manner. Two others are quarrelling, one having just spouted a mouthful of wine in the face of the other who, in retaliation, has drawn a knife and is holding it threateningly. A black woman is shown laughing as she watches them. This reflects an incident supposedly witnessed by Hogarth. J T Smith records that Hogarth and his friend Francis Hayman, the painter, were visiting Moll King's Coffee House and

53. *A Rake's Progress* III, *The Orgy*, engraving, first state. (The Royal Collection © 2007, Her Majesty Queen Elizabeth II)

54. *A Rake's Progress* III, engraving, third state

55. William Hogarth, *An Evening at the Rose Tavern, Scene III*, 1832–34, oil on canvas. (The Nelson-Atkins Museum of Art, Kansas City, Missouri. Purchase: Nelson Trust, 56-2. Photograph by Robert Newcombe)

witnessed two women quarrelling, one of whom spat wine or gin straight into her adversary's face.

Musicians are entertaining the company with a triple harp, decorated with the figure of King David, and a trumpet, a rather strange combination of instruments. The triple harp was probably made by David Evans whose workshop was actually in Rose Court, Covent Garden (a harp bearing his label and the date 1736 is in the Victoria and Albert Museum). They are accompanying (or possibly competing with) the ballad singer who is standing in the doorway performing a bawdy song called 'Black Joke'. Leather Coat, the porter at the Rose Tavern, brings in a large salver, inscribed 'At the Rose Tavern Drury Lane, John Bonvine' (a play on the French *bon vin* or *bon viv[r]e*: good wine or good living). Leather Coat was famous for the strength of his ribs and for a pot of beer would lie in the road and let a carriage wheel run over him. The 'posture woman' in the left foreground is stripping and will shortly perform on the salver, adopting various obscene postures for the entertainment of the clients. In *The Rake's Progress or The Humours of Drury Lane: A Poem*, London, 1735, inspired by Hogarth, these lines appear –

> Now Leathersides,[21] who's apt to wait,
> Shews him the consecrated Plate,
> In which the Fair, the Black, the Brown
> By Turns have Nature's Beauties shewn.

Jean André Rouquet, describing the engravings for a French friend in 1746, gave a detailed description of such performances, adding that houses such as this were common in London; also that the Rose Tavern, with its mirror, map and paintings of the Caesars, makes a pretence at elegance but the faces of all the Caesars, except the notorious Nero (who famously watched Rome burn after a night of debauchery), have been mutilated.

The setting for this lively scene is one of squalor. The mirror is broken, so are some of the chairs. Wine is spilt on the table and floor; glasses and bottles lie all over the place. A brimming chamber pot (lower left corner) has been knocked over next to food set down on the floor, some of which has fallen off a plate. The posture woman's fancy stocking is full of holes. The detail of a prostitute holding a candle dangerously near to the map of the globe (*Totus mundus*) on the wall is in fact a prophecy: Tom's world will indeed go up in flames.[22]

The early states of the engravings are very close to the painting (Fig. 53) but in the third state (Fig. 54) several changes are made, including the hat on the girl fondling the Rake and the way her accomplice receives the stolen watch. The torn painting in the frame on the left is replaced by an undamaged one of a fat man labelled 'Pontac', who was, according to Ireland, 'an eminent cook, whose great talents being turned to heightening the corporeal rather than the mental enjoyments . . . has a much better chance of a votive offering from this company, than would either Vespasian or Trajan'.

Hogarth's *An Evening at the Rose Tavern* (Fig. 55), a painting in the Nelson-Atkins Museum of Art, in Kansas City, seems to be a preparatory sketch for the *Orgy* scene in the Soane, but it is painted in a summary manner, in no way worked over and finished. Tavern scenes and scenes of rather boisterous meals had been a favourite theme with painters in seventeenth-century Holland and had long been an accepted genre of painting.

SCENE IV: THE ARREST

This scene (Fig. 56) shows an elegantly dressed Tom Rakewell, on his way to a reception at St James's Palace to celebrate Queen Caroline's birthday, where he will mix with the highest ranks of Society. He has hired a sedan chair numbered 41. As on similar royal occasions today, a traffic jam has built up and the street is blocked by carriages and other sedan chairs. The background is a topographical view of St James's Palace looking down St James's Street and the buildings depicted include White's Chocolate House, which was well known also for its use as a gaming house. The clock in the background shows the time as twenty to two. The Queen was born on 1 March, St David's day, and so two of the men wear leeks in their hats to mark the occasion.

56. *A Rake's Progress* IV: *The Arrest*

In his pursuit of pleasure Tom has spent all his inheritance and the fact that he has hired a sedan-chair and kept the curtains drawn suggests that he is anticipating trouble and had hoped to reach the Court undetected. There he might perhaps find a patron who would rescue him from his financial embarrassments, an ironic reversal of his own *levée* in Scene II. However, he is stopped and arrested for debt by two bailiffs before he can reach this haven – they are aiming to present him at a different kind of 'court' from the one he is anticipating. In his surprise Tom drops his gold-headed cane which is seized by a passing urchin. The sturdy watchman on the right (with his hands tucked into a muff for warmth) looks on with grim approval at the consequences of folly and ostentation and the idiotic-looking lamplighter is so engrossed in the scene that he overfills the lamp and the oil spills on to the Rake's wig below.

Sarah Young, Tom's discarded mistress, witnesses the arrest and rushes forward, buying off the bailiffs by offering her purse which presumably contains her hard-earned wages; the ribbons and caps falling from the box inscribed with her name show that she is now working as a milliner. Her gesture, offering her purse to rescue Tom, echoes and parodies his action in Scene I in trying to buy her off with a handful of coins. Parallels can be drawn with the biblical story of the angel intervening as Abraham is about to sacrifice Isaac and it has been suggested that the oil falling

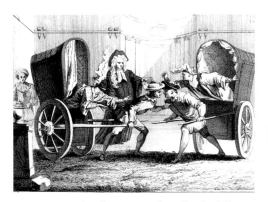

57. Jacques-Gabriel Huquier, after Claude Gillot, *La Scène des Carrosses*, engraving. (Bibliothèque nationale de France)

58. *A Rake's Progress* IV, *The Arrest*, engraving, first state. (The Royal Collection © 2007, Her Majesty Queen Elizabeth II)

59. *A Rake's Progress* IV, engraving, first state revised. (Courtesy of The Lewis Walpole Library, Yale University)

60. *A Rake's Progress* IV, engraving, second state. (Courtesy of The Lewis Walpole Library, Yale University)

61. *A Rake's Progress* IV, engraving, third state

on to the Rake's head is a quasi-religious reference to anointing. Sarah is cast as an angel of mercy.

The composition, with the Rake starting forward out of the sedan-chair, is thought to be influenced by Claude Gillot's painting *La Scène des Carrosses*, which Hogarth probably knew from Huquier's engraved rendering (Fig. 57). As Gillot was depicting a scene from a play, the postures are rather over-dramatised.

The engraved version of *The Arrest* was worked on by Hogarth more than any other. In the painting there is blue sky with soft white clouds, while golden light and strong shadows suggest that the sun is shining. The first state of the engraving (Fig. 58) is very like the painting but a retouched copy exists (Fig. 59) in which Hogarth has inked in storm clouds and a passing shower in the background and has given Sarah a hat rather than a cap. In the second state (Fig. 60) different storm clouds and a streak of lightning have been etched in, the bolt of lightning, suggestive of divine judgement, aiming directly at White's as if to emphasize that it is a den of iniquity. On the right-hand side the single urchin has been replaced by a group of seven urchins on a raised pavement, playing cards and thus emphasizing the theme of gambling. One of the boys is stealing a handkerchief from the Rake's pocket, echoing the actions of the prostitute in the previous scene. A sign inscribed 'WHITES' is placed outside the chocolate house; a post inscribed 'BLACK' is placed behind the group of boys on the extreme right, thus directly contrasting them and their gambling with that of the upper classes in White's. The saddler's sign directly above Tom's head reminds us of his connection with horseracing. In the third state (Fig. 61) the curtain of the sedan-chair is only partly drawn, the storm has been changed again and this time the foreground has also been darkened so that the storm seems more directly overhead. By the time this final state is reached, the engraving shows considerable changes from the painting.

SCENE V: THE MARRIAGE

Sarah's intervention to save him from prison has by no means made Tom turn to her in gratitude and repentance. Rather, he seeks to recoup his fortunes by marrying an elderly spinster (Fig. 62). She may only have one eye but is very wealthy. The law of the time gave a husband complete control over his wife's property, so he is willing to overlook her lack of beauty. He does not, however, think it inappropriate to eye up her pretty young maid during the wedding ceremony. On the other hand he pays no attention to Sarah who is holding their child. She, the child and her mother are in the background, being prevented from entering the church to try to stop the ceremony. The parson and his clerk appear unperturbed by the interruption although the fracas has attracted the attention of a man in the gallery.

The bride's eye gleams in anticipation and this grotesque detail is echoed in the one-eyed bitch seated on a stool to the right who receives the attention of a pug dog who is probably a portrait of Hogarth's own dog, Pugg. The white patch on the bitch's front is paralleled in the bride's exaggerated décolletage. The evergreen decorations may be intended to suggest Christmas or to indicate that at least nine months have passed (an allusion to Tom's fathering of Sarah's child), or they may simply be a comment on the wintry age of the bride.

62. A Rake's Progress V: The Marriage

The building is recognisable from the architecture and memorial inscriptions as Marylebone Old Church, which, being then on the outskirts of London, was a popular place for hurried or clandestine weddings. On the right can be seen an inscription that 'This Church of / St Mary le Bone / was Beautifyed / in the Year 1725 / Thos Horn, Thos Sice / Church Wardens'; yet already it is in a very dilapidated state demonstrating perhaps not just the decay of the building but the failure of the Church as an institution to offer any alternative to a life of vice. Messrs Sice and Horn were indeed church-wardens in 1725 when the repairs were made, but maybe Hogarth wishes to suggest that the 'Beautifying' was done poorly and cheaply. Plaster is falling from the walls, the pulpit is stained, the kneeler before the dogs is torn and the poor-box opening is covered by a spider's web which suggests that the donations are very few. The parish boy who is placing the kneeler wears a coat and shoes which are full of holes. On the right, behind the parson, are boards inscribed with the Creed and the Ten Commandments but the former has a large section missing and the latter a great crack running across it.

In Scene I Tom rejected the idea of marriage with the young and pretty Sarah. In the *Levée* Hogarth mockingly compared Tom to Paris, who chose Venus, the goddess of love, in a contest, having been promised the most beautiful woman in the world. Now, in this Scene, we see Tom's 'Helen of Troy' in the form of his ageing, one-eyed and grotesque bride.

The first state of the engraving (Fig. 63) is close to the painting but in later states Hogarth changes the appearance of the bridesmaid to make her look less like Sarah and her cap is slightly changed (Fig. 64). One detail which is no longer visible on the painting, though faint marks suggest it was originally present, is the IHS within a circle on the pulpit which provides a halo behind the elderly bride's head.

63. *A Rake's Progress* V, engraving, first state. (The Royal Collection © 2007, Her Majesty Queen Elizabeth II)

SCENE VI: THE GAMING HOUSE

Tom Rakewell has learnt nothing and dissipates this second fortune as he did the first. He has just gambled away the last of it and is seen in the foreground gesturing in despair and cursing Heaven. In his frenzy he has thrown off his wig and overturned his chair, across which a black dog, a traditional symbol of depressive melancholy, barks at him (Fig. 65 p.44). He is not the only loser and elsewhere in the painting Hogarth shows other reactions of those unlucky at the tables. Behind the dog is a man convulsed with despair and pulling his hat down to hide his face. He is dressed in mourning which suggests that the money he has lost is a very recent inheritance. On the extreme right a nobleman bears his losses more tranquilly and is borrowing money from a usurer to continue his gambling. The nobleman is said to resemble 'Old Manners', a relative of the Duke of Rutland, who amassed a fortune from gambling. The usurer, a finely drawn character, records the transaction 'Lent to L[or]d Cogg 500'. In the centre background another gambler shrinks in fear from a demented loser, who looks even wilder than the Rake and brandishes his sword at the cowering man, possibly accusing him of cheating. His attack is impeded by a drunken man who staggers against him. The two figures sharing profits on the left suggest that there may have been a certain amount of collusion and dishonest play. The main winner seems to be the large man behind the Rake, seen gathering up his winnings. The figure on the left, (being offered a drink), may well be a highwayman judging by the pistols and mask hanging from his pocket. From his gloomy demeanour it looks as if he has also lost money: in his introspection he does not notice the boy who has brought him a drink. On the extreme left, behind the boy, another loser leans against the wall and clenches his arms around himself in despair.

64. *A Rake's Progress* V, engraving, third state

The prophetic allusion in Scene III (*The Orgy*) to fire is here fulfilled. The gamblers have been so engrossed in their play that they have not noticed that the house is on fire; even when a watchman with a lantern and staff (similar to the ones acquired by Tom in Scene III) rushes in to raise the alarm, they are still so absorbed that they pay no attention. Of the sixteen people in the room, only two, including a croupier holding a money rake and a tall staff topped with lighted candles, pay any attention to the

66. *A Rake's Progress* VI, engraving, third state

65. *A Rake's Progress* VI: *The Gaming House*

smoke which is billowing into the room just below the ceiling at the back. As White's Chocolate House in St James's Street was destroyed by fire on 3 May 1733 it has been suggested that the scene is set there. However, the room seems rather dingy and undistinguished for White's and the inscription on the dog's collar 'Covent Gar . . .' perhaps indicates a location in Covent Garden. Jean André Rouquet, in his comments on the engravings, says that the grille in front of the fireplace was usual in gaming houses to prevent unlucky players injuring themselves in their despair.

In this case the engraving is very close to the painting in all its states, the only significant differences being the suggestion of flames as well as smoke (Fig. 66 p.43).

SCENE VII: THE PRISON

Unable to pay his debts, Tom has been confined in The Fleet, a prison for debtors (Fig. 67). Like many other debtors he has devised a scheme to extricate himself from his embarrassments, in his case by writing a play; counting on money to be made from its successful production he has ordered various comforts from the gaoler. However his play has just been rejected and returned. It lies tied up in a bundle on the table beside him with the words 'Act 4', visible and a note 'Sir I have read your Play & find it will not doe yrs J R . . . h.'. This is undoubtedly a reference to John Rich (1692–1761), the manager of the Covent Garden Theatre who put on John Gay's *The Beggar's Opera* with such success. Hogarth had made several paintings of a scene from *The Beggar's Opera*,

67. A Rake's Progress VII: The Prison

68. *A Rake's Progress* VII, engraving, third state

set in a prison, a few years previously. Tom is now unable to pay his prison fees and the gaoler is pointing to the careful record he has kept in his book under the heading 'Garnish money'. Moreover the boy is refusing to hand over the drink Tom has ordered unless he is paid.

Tom's wife, now reduced to penury by her profligate husband, screams at him. Her dishevelled appearance and costume show how she has suffered from her foolish marriage; she was previously plump but now appears emaciated. Her angry gesture apes that of her husband in the previous scene. Sarah has come to visit Tom in prison accompanied by their child and by her mother, but she is so overcome by the horror of his plight that she has fainted. Her mother tries to revive her by slapping her hands while another woman waves smelling salts under her nose. They have already loosened her stays. The child is upset and clings to her skirts, on the verge of tears. Tom's expression shows complete despair and suggests he has moved further along the road to insanity.

Each of the other prisoners has his own scheme for improving his finances or for escaping from prison. The man in the background is an alchemist, trying to change base metal into gold. Draped over the four-poster bed is a pair of wings, made by a prisoner in the hope of using them to fly out of the prison. On the extreme right, helping to support Sarah, is a man who has dropped some papers, on one page of which is written 'Being a New Scheme for Paying ye Debts of ye Nation by T.L. now a prisoner in the Fleet'. Other inmates have been seeking solace from the stars to judge by the telescope poking out through the small grille. On a piece of paper projecting from the book on the shelf above the gaoler's head is written 'On ye Philosophers' Stone'. The engravings are close to the painting (Fig. 68) though one early state lacks some of the inscriptions.

SCENE VIII: THE MADHOUSE

The last two scenes have depicted Tom's mind gradually giving way and now he is confined in the mad-house (Fig. 69). The most famous mad-house of the time was the Royal Bethlehem Hospital, known as 'Bedlam', in Moorfields, just outside the wall of the City of London. It was an impressive building completed in 1676 to the designs of Robert Hooke (1635–1703) and its entrance gates were adorned with two reclining statues by Caius Gabriel Cibber depicting 'Melancholy Madness' and 'Raving Madness', *c*.1675 (Figs 70 and 71).

Tom is seen lying in the foreground, shackled and almost naked (Fig. 72). Despite the suffering he has brought her, which is shown in her careworn face, Sarah is still faithful and weeps for his plight. Behind them, bending forward, stands a figure who is probably the mad-house keeper. Another attendant adjusts the fetters on Tom's legs. The scene has been interpreted both as Tom being shackled after a fit of raging madness and as him being unshackled as he is near death. The presence of a patch on his right breast in the engravings suggests that he may have wounded himself in such a fit and perhaps that the wound was so serious that he is on the point of death. Bakewell says 'Having attempted to lay violent Hands on himself, as appears by the Wound in his Side, they are obliged to chain him. He is afterwards confin'd down to his Bed in a dark Room, where he miserably expires.' The group of four figures forms a pyramid and

69. *A Rake's Progress* VIII: *The Madhouse*

echoes a standard composition for the 'Lamentation for the Dead Christ' with Sarah playing the part of the bereaved Virgin. Tom's own position echoes that of Cibber's statue of 'Raving Madness' (Fig. 71). Beside Sarah is a cauldron of the milk porridge with which those confined in Bedlam were fed.

The religious maniac in cell 54 behind the Rake (to the right) is depicted in the same pose as Cibber's 'Melancholy Madness' (Fig. 70); he looks up in a fever of exaltation at a cross. Behind him on the wall are three pictures which cannot be identified. This figure, with his bed of straw-covered stone and the bowl lying in front of it (best seen in the engravings, see Figs 74–76), also recalls many traditional depictions of hermits.

In cell 55 (centre) a naked man, imagining he is a king, wears a crown of straw and

70–71. Caius Gabriel Cibber: *Melancholy Madness* and *Raving Madness*, 1680 (Photographs: Guildhall Library, City of London)

holds a stick as a sceptre. He is urinating against the wall of his cell, to the amusement of the two fashionable ladies who are visiting Bedlam to pass an idle hour (Fig. 73). One peers at him from behind her fan while her companion whispers in her ear. They find the behaviour of the lunatics a source only of merriment. It is a final irony that while Tom set out to ape the aristocratic lifestyle he ends by being one of its entertainments. Their lack of feeling is in contrast to Sarah's grief and compassion for the man who has betrayed her.

The space between cells 54 and 55 is not easy to read in the painting as Hogarth seems to have done much reworking and some of the rejected ideas show through the layers of paint. It seems likely that Hogarth's final version resembled what is shown in the earliest stages of the engraving (see Fig. 74); close to the door of cell 55 a man is drawing lines upon the wall to represent a scheme for discovering longitude by the firing of bombs; in front of him is a man who peers at the ceiling through a rolled paper imitating a telescope as if studying the stars. In front of cell 55 is a lunatic tailor who twists a tape-measure frantically in his hands and wears a hat in which are fixed a series of patterns and has straw twined in his hair.

It is possible to see, even with the naked eye, in a raking light, that the king from cell 55 was once placed between cells 54 and 55: he still holds a rod but instead of a straw crown he wears an upturned pitcher on his head. The man drawing longitude seems to be partly drawn over another figure in full wig and robe who seems more likely to be an attendant or the mad-house keeper than an inmate. Facing the door frame of cell 54 is a third figure missing from the engraving; as he is close to the drawing of the bomb in the diagram for determining longitude he may be Hogarth's first design for the prisoner drawing longitude.

On the left is a group which includes a mad musician who wears a score on his head as he fiddles away. A religious maniac under the delusion he is a pope intones some

72. *A Rake's Progress* VIII, detail

73. *A Rake's Progress* VIII, detail

74. *A Rake's Progress* VIII, engraving, first state. (The Royal Collection © 2007, Her Majesty Queen Elizabeth II)

75. *A Rake's Progress* VIII, engraving, second state. (The Royal Collection © 2007, Her Majesty Queen Elizabeth II)

76. *A Rake's Progress* VIII, engraving, third state

anthem as he holds an elaborate cross and wears a tall paper hat decorated with crosses. This inclusion of this figure may allude to the corruption and superstition often associated with the papacy at this time. In front a melancholic, seated on the staircase, clasps his hands together and gazes into space, while a small dog similar to the one in *The Gaming House* barks at him.

Much of the detail is clearer in the engravings (Figs 74–76). One can see that both crosses have been made by nailing or tying pieces of wood together and that the paintings at the back of cell 54 depict Saints; they are labelled 'Clement(i)', 'St Athanatius' and 'St Lawrence'. An inscription on the stair-rail, 'Charming Betty Careless', makes it clear that the melancholic has become deranged through his hopeless love for the beautiful courtesan whose portrait he wears around his neck. He may be a depiction of William Ellis who was believed to have become insane as a result of love for 'Miss Betty Careless', a famous actress and prostitute who played 'Polly' in Gay's *Beggar's Opera* and died in 1752.

Two early states of engraving are close to the painting but many of the figures are unfinished and much of the lettering has not yet been added. In the third state (Fig. 76), which was retouched by Hogarth in 1763, he has added the reverse of a 1763 halfpenny to the wall between cells 55 and 54; it is inscribed BRITANNIA but the usual depiction of that figure has been changed to one with wildly flying hair, suggesting that Britannia herself is demented. In the same state Hogarth alters the headgear of the lady with the fan from a hood to a hat and makes her look away from the urinating king towards her friend whose face is now in shadow. The man behind Tom and Sarah now wears clerical bands rather than an open shirt so that he seems to have become a cleric rather than an official of the mad-house. This reinforces the interpretation that Tom is on the point of death; the accompanying verses include the line 'Behold Death grappling with despair'.

Description of the four paintings and the engravings of An Election

SCENE I: AN ELECTION ENTERTAINMENT

In May 1754 *The London Magazine* reported that since the Election date had been announced 'nothing has been . . . thought of but feasting and revelling; and both parties strive to outdo each other in the expense of their entertainments'.[23] The first painting of *An Election* (Fig. 77) shows just such a 'treat' given by the Whigs (identified by their orange rosettes) to gain the support of voters. The scene recalls a description in an 'Old Interest' propaganda pamphlet of a feast held at the strongly pro-Whig Exeter College in Oxford:

> the pictures in hall were offuscated [sic = obfuscated] with such Clouds of Tobacco-smoke, as sharper and stronger Eyes than mine would not have been able to penetrate. In one Corner of the Room I observed Men and Women embracing, in another spitting and sp . . . ing, in another descanting upon the Good-Nature and Affability of Mr. ****, and the forcible Eloquence of Mr. ****; at the same Time regaling themselves with Pipes and Tobacco, and a huge Tankard of mild Ale.

A mass of humanity is seen in a large room at an inn. One can almost smell the alcohol and perspiration, feel the close, hot atmosphere and hear the din of the musicians. The composition is skilful and dazzlingly complex, with a mass of figures gathered round two tables, all seen from a high viewpoint.

The slashed portrait on the wall (to the left of the window) is of King William III, the Dutch Protestant who supplanted James II in the Glorious Revolution of 1688, ruling England jointly with his wife, Mary II, until her death in 1694. The damage to the picture may have been done during a previous Tory 'treat' as William would have been abhorred by any voter with Jacobite leanings.

Drink flows freely; in the foreground a pot boy is mixing punch in a large tub. Further left a corpulent Quaker is examining with great care a note reading 'April 1754 / I promise to pay to / . . . of 20 pounds six / months after date / R Pention'. He seems doubtful about accepting this post-dated promise in payment for various gifts and favours which he has been asked to supply.

Moving round the picture clockwise we come, just above him, to one of the two candidates, wearing a blue coat and with a somewhat pained expression, suffering the embraces of a fat old woman. The man behind encourages the embrace while setting the candidate's wig alight with the embers from his pipe. While the candidate is thus occupied a young girl examines the ring on his finger, probably intending to steal it. This candidate is said to be a portrait of a contemporary MP, Thomas Potter (1718?–1759), who was associated with Sir Francis Dashwood's notorious 'Monks of

77. An Election I: An Election Entertainment

Medmenham Abbey' (often now referred to as the 'Hellfire Club'), who were commonly thought to hold orgiastic and satanic meetings at the ruined Medmenham Abbey in Buckinghamshire. The second candidate, seated behind him, in an olive green coat, is enduring the maudlin attentions of two drunks, one of whom grasps his hand while the other leans across him and puffs smoke in his face. In the composition, there seems to be a parallel between these figures and those of Judas, St Peter and St John in Leonardo's *Last Supper*. The candidates are distinguished by the laurels attached to their chairs and by the orange banner inscribed 'LIBERTY and LOYALTY' behind them. In the background, by the window, a soldier and a pretty girl are conversing and some object is changing hands. Another drunken man serenades them, clasping one of the soldier's hands and holding his glass in a perilous manner above the girl's head.

A gross parson seems to be the only person still eating. The heat from the chafing dish in front of him makes him sweat and he has taken off his wig to mop his bald head. Next to him a long-chinned gentleman is pinching the equally long chin of one of the musicians (Fig. 79). The other three musicians, who form the apex of the human composition under the portrait of William III, are a woman with a viol, said to be a portrait of 'Fiddling Nan' who was well known in Oxfordshire, and two men with a cello and a pair of bagpipes. Silhouetted against the cello are three figures, shown reacting to events in the room. Two are amused by the collapse of the mayor (to the right, at the head of the table) while the third is cowering back from the missiles flying in through the window. In the street outside the Tory party is holding a procession and some of their supporters are hurling bricks at the opposing party. One man fends these off with a stool while another empties the contents of a chamber pot over the Tories. Tory banners railing against Whig-promised initiatives are visible through the window. 'MARRY AND MULTIPLY IN SPITE OF THE DEVIL' refers to a recent Marriage Bill directed against irregular marriages. Tory supporters also carry an effigy labelled 'No Jews', symbol of a popular campaign launched by the Tories against the Whigs' 'Jew Bill' of 1753, which granted a limited number of Jewish merchants exemption from the Christian oath when applying for naturalisation. The Tories prophesied a massive influx of Jews and a gradual Jewish takeover of all national institutions. The outcry was so great that the government had to repeal the Act six months later. The effigy may be that of the Duke of Newcastle who supported the Act.

78. *An Election* I, detail

Beneath the window a man with his wig askew is attempting to amuse his companion by singing 'An Old Woman Clothed in Gray', illustrating it with the aid of his napkin and a face drawn on his hand.[24] This figure, according to Hogarth, is a portrait of John Parnell, a well known Dublin attorney, who asked to be included in the painting. His companion seems to be suffering from a severe attack of gout or 'gravel' and is not impressed by his performance.

At the far end of the table (to the right) the Mayor is about to be bled by a barber-surgeon: he has collapsed following a surfeit of oysters (Fig. 80). Behind him stands a man who is actually refusing a bribe, with his hands folded as if in prayer, although his wife urges him to take it while his son is pointing out that he needs some new shoes. Behind them three men armed with clubs and swords are repelling Tory supporters who are attempting to break into the room. In the lower right-hand corner the Election agent has just been hit by a flying brick and is falling backwards (Fig. 80). He has been keeping a list of 'Sure Votes', which seems to have only one entry, and 'Doubtful [votes]', which has many. The pile of plates and food beside his chair is delicately painted, resembling a miniature still life (Fig. 78). Moving to the left we see a man whose head has been injured in a fight with members of the opposing party, during which he has captured one of their banners inscribed 'Give us our/Eleven Days'. This refers to the fact that when Britain finally adopted the Gregorian calendar in 1752 it was necessary to omit eleven days and pass straight from 3 September to 14 September. Many people objected to the new calendar as popish and others thought they would actually lose eleven days from their lives. The father of Lord Parker, the Whig candidate, was Lord Macclesfield, astronomer and President of the Royal Society, who had helped prepare this change of calendar, so the whole question was an especially live issue in the Oxfordshire campaign. The injured man is being treated with gin externally and internally: while he drains a glass a butcher holds a piece of paper inscribed '. . . and vote /. . [o]ld Interest' [i.e. Tory] to his head and pours alcohol over both.

The engravings after this painting are not reversed and Hogarth seems to have had

79. *An Election* I, detail

80. *An Election* I, detail

considerable trouble in producing a plate which he found acceptable, judging by the large number of states. The first state is unusual in that it differs in some respects from both the painting and the other states (Fig. 81): there is no door behind the parson who is mopping his head and the oval behind the stag's antlers is in a very narrow frame which contains a mirror. The painting and all later states have a door; there is a wider frame and no reflection. By the fourth state the oval has become an actual opening in the wall. The first three states show several lemons lying on a piece of paper near the punch-tub and on the table above the tub there is a piece of bread beside the salt cellar (both disappear in the fourth state). A lettered ribbon is added to the headgear of the butcher reading 'FOR OUR COUNTRY' which is altered in the fourth state to 'PRO PATRIA'. A wine glass is added on the table behind his chair and in the fourth state this is filled with a dark liquid. The inscription on the banners outside the window is slightly changed and rearranged. The butcher pours the alcohol from a bottle labelled 'GIN' directly on his patient's head – there is no piece of paper. The note held by the Quaker is longer and more legible 'April 1 1754 / I promise to Pay to Abel / Squat the sum of Fifty / pounds six months after / date Value . . . ved / Rich . . . Slim'. The escutcheon on the wall has been made more telling: it is suspended from an open mouth and seems to include three coins, probably guineas, and has the motto 'Speak and Have'. There is also a note in front of the second candidate 'To / Sir Commodity / Taxem'; the hand holding it belongs either to that candidate or to the fat woman. In the bottom right corner is a tray of pipes with a tin of tobacco labelled 'Kirton Best'. Kirton was a tobacconist in Fleet Street who ruined himself in the Oxfordshire election. In the fourth state the fat woman loses her one remaining tooth and the Puritan is identified as a tailor by the scissors hanging from his belt. In the early states the agent's book suggests many names on the 'Sure Votes' page and one or none under 'Doubtful' but in the fourth state this is reversed as in the painting. In the fifth state an extra hat is added in the left foreground and windows have been added to the house seen behind the procession. Other changes are made in later states (see Fig. 82).

81. *An Election* I, engraving, first state.
(© Copyright the Trustees of The British Museum)

82. *An Election* I, engraving, eighth state.
(© Copyright the Trustees of The British Museum)

SCENE II: CANVASSING FOR VOTES

The second scene takes place in the street of a small country town (Fig. 83). The main buildings visible are three inns, the Royal Oak in the foreground, the Crown behind and the Portobello to the right of the painting. In the distance is a finely painted sky and landscape. The landlady is seated by the door of the Royal Oak, counting the money they have made from 'treats' held at the inn. A soldier eyes the money enviously from the doorway. Her seat is the figurehead of a ship showing the British lion eating a French fleur-de-lys, a reminder of the fact that France and Britain were at war during much of this period. 'Treating' seems to be going on both at the Royal Oak (see Fig. 84) and at the Crown as in the centre foreground a stout young countryman is being bribed by the landlords of both these establishments, acting as agents for the rival parties. Each is placing coins in one hand and proffering an invitation: these read 'Your Company to / Dine at the Royal Oak' and '. . . / at the Crown'. He slyly looks to see which offer is the larger and seems to favour the bribe of the Royal Oak; he is also perhaps influenced by the landlord's girth which suggests more and better food is to be had at that establishment. The composition reflects that of the traditional subject of the Choice of Hercules

83. *An Election II: Canvassing for Votes*

84. *An Election* II, detail

(Hercules at the Crossroads choosing between Virtue and Pleasure). *A Political Description of Mr. Hogarth's Election Prints in Four Cantos written under Mr. Hogarth's Sanction and Inspection*, London, 1759, includes the following verse:

> Which Party shall the Voter take,
> Since both the same Pretensions make?
> The same? – sure not – for see each Hand!
> Ay now he seems to understand:
> The Crown Host fees him o'er his Arm;
> But t'other tips the stronger Charm.
> But don't exalt; for being loth
> To disoblige, he's taken from both.[25]

The Royal Oak, the name of which commemorates Charles II's escape after the battle of Worcester, is appropriately the inn being used by the Tory party. Its yard is to be used to stage an anti-government play or puppet show and a sign publicising this half obscures the painting of the Royal Oak. The new sign shows gold pouring from a window of the Treasury and being laden into a wagon labelled 'OXFORD'; thereafter it is distributed from a wheelbarrow to voters by 'PUNCH CANDIDATE FOR GUZZLEDOWN'. Two bags of coin are labelled '9000 L' and '700 . . .'. The play will obviously suggest that the ruling party, the Whigs, have been using money raised by taxation to pay for election expenses and bribes. The building on the left in the upper part of the sign is the Horse Guards on Whitehall, designed by William Kent (1686–1748), a painter and architect whom Hogarth despised. When this building was first erected it was criticised for the lowness of its arch. Here Hogarth shows the royal coachman's head being knocked off as he drives through the opening and he has replaced the cupola of the building with a beer barrel. Beneath the window of the Royal Oak a kneeling man is trying to deliver to the Tory agent two parcels of handbills for the play as well as some election pamphlets. Examples of the contents are attached to the boxes 'AT PUNCHES THEAT . . ./ IN THE ROYAL / OKE YARD' and 'Sir Your Vote /. . . & Interest'. The agent's name appears on the bill the man is holding out, 'Tim^y / Partitool Esq'. However, the agent is at the moment occupied in purchasing from a Jewish pedlar gifts for two ladies on the balcony, presumably hoping they will influence their relatives to vote Tory.

85. *An Election* II, engraving, first state.
(© Copyright the Trustees of The British Museum)

Further down the street the Crown Inn, which is the scene of the rival Whig 'treat' is being besieged by an angry crowd, protesting against government taxation. One man is busily cutting down the sign of the Crown, apparently not realising that he is seated on the part that will fall when he has sawn through the beam. A gun is fired at the mob from an upper window.

In the right foreground, at the Portobello, a barber with a basin and a cobbler are enjoying a drink and a smoke; they are recalling, nostalgically, how Admiral Vernon captured Portobello in 1739 with only six ships. The barber uses pieces of clay pipe to explain the plan of battle. This allusion to a past British naval victory against the French, together with the debasement of the patriotic figurehead opposite (now a humble bench) is intended to underline a current decline in Britain's international fortunes, presided over by a corrupt political elite. In the last (sixth) state of the engraved version (by which time Britain was doing badly in the Seven Years War and had lost Minorca to the French) Hogarth removed the teeth from the British lion. The barber's tankard is inscribed 'John Storr / Porto Bell'. Beneath the inn sign, depicting ships, is written 'PORTO B . . .'.

86. *An Election* II, engraving, third state.
(© Copyright the Trustees of The British Museum)

The early states of the engraving of *Canvassing for Votes* are interesting as they show how an engraver would work on a plate. In this case the plate was not engraved by Hogarth but by Charles Grignion (1754–1804), one of the *emigré* French artists moving in the same circles as Hogarth, Hayman, Roubilliac, Gravelot and Moser. The first state is a proof in which most of the figures, the Punch sign, the framework of the inn on the left and the pavement are only partly finished (Fig. 85). The sky remains untouched but most of the other background has been finished. Note, however, that a narrow area of unfinished background is usually left adjoining the heads of important figures. The inscriptions are all missing; they were usually added last. In the second (proof) state more work was done on the pavement and on the framework of the Portobello. By the third state (Fig. 86) the engraving looks more finished although the lower part of the sky is still untouched and in the group on the left the landlady and the Agent's face are still incomplete as is the old woman on the left of the Punch sign. There is still

87. *An Election* II, engraving, sixth state.
(© Copyright the Trustees of The British Museum)

an un-worked strip of background next to the face of the figure on the left of the central group. The inscriptions are still lacking. These were added in the fourth and fifth states. The lion's teeth were removed in the final, sixth, state, as we have just noted (Fig. 87). The reversal from the painting means that the Portobello Inn, with part of its sign visible ('TOBELLO') is now on the left. The final state of the engraving is very close to the painting, with no significant changes other than minor alterations to the inscriptions.

SCENE III: THE POLLING

This scene shows the election in progress with a polling booth in the foreground and a superb atmospheric landscape in the background (Figs 88 and 89). The flags of the two parties fly over the booth and two candidates can be seen seated on high chairs at the

88 An Election III: *The Polling*

back of the booth. One candidate, presumably the Whig as he is near the orange flag, seems calm and satisfied leaning on his cane; the other is worried by the way the election is going and mops his brow. Between them the constable has fallen asleep, clutching his staff of office. On the extreme right a caricaturist is causing some amusement with his depiction of one of the candidates. Near the Tory candidate a group of men are reading and enjoying a broadsheet which they have just bought from an old woman. No text is visible but judging by the gallows at the top of the page it is probably suggesting that one of the candidates merits such a fate. A motley group of voters make their way up the steps to record their votes. There was of course no secret ballot in the eighteenth century and electors (male freeholders of land worth 40 shillings a year or more) recorded their votes openly for the party of their choice; if challenged they had to take an oath affirming their right to vote. This is evidently causing some difficulty here for the first voter is a soldier who has lost both hands and one leg in the service of his country. He has no hand to lay on the Bible in order to take the oath and one lawyer is suggesting he is therefore disenfranchised, which is being disputed by the other lawyer who feels his hook is a suitable substitute. Behind him an idiot is about to register his vote. He seems unlikely to be able to comprehend the issues involved but is prompted loudly by the man who has carried his chair to the polling booth. This man wears fetters on his legs and has presumably escaped from prison. Behind these two a grey-faced man wrapped in a blanket is carried up the steps by two men, one with a livid red face. The grey-faced man seems close to death but has none the less been brought out to record his vote. Behind is a blind man and a hunch-back. In a brilliant pictorial device four staves are shown at the lower right edge of the picture, implying a further group of supporters standing below the raised booth.

On the stone bridge in the background is a scene of chaos as those arriving to vote meet those who are leaving, and it seems that fighting has broken out. It may be that supporters of one party are trying to prevent electors of the other party from reaching the polling booth, as did in fact happen in the Oxfordshire election. A mob appears to be surrounding a coach. Here, Hogarth is likely to be referring to a recent incident on Magdalen Bridge in Oxford, when a Tory mob surrounded a Whig post-chaise and threatened to topple it. The siege ended when a Captain Turton shot dead a Tory chimney-sweep, dispersing the mob. In the next painting, *Chairing the Member*, the chimney-sweeps will have their revenge.

The sense of a nation being failed by its political leaders is made even more explicit in *The Polling* than it was in the previous scene. On the left Britannia's coach (Fig. 90), with the Union Flag of England and Scotland painted on the door, has just broken down and the horses are plunging about wildly: a reference perhaps to the white stallions of the ruling house of Hanover. The coachmen – allegorical representations of the country's leaders – seem not to care and do not respond to the attempts of the female passenger to gain their attention. They are engrossed in a game of cards at which one seems to be cheating. Hogarth thus suggests that those entrusted with the welfare of Britannia are deaf to her needs and pursue only their own corrupt pleasures and interests.

In the first (proof) state the engraving is very close to the painting but many of the faces are only lightly sketched in (Fig. 91). The clerk administering the soldier's oath hides his mouth with his hand as if to disguise amusement at the strange situation. One of the two men carrying the sick man has no nose, as if it had been eaten away by some disease, and the other has some sort of growth on his nose. The blind man wears

89. *An Election* III, detail

90. *An Election* III, detail

91. *An Election* III, engraving, first state.
(© Copyright the Trustees of The British Museum)

a bandage over his eyes. The inscriptions appear in the third state, often with topical allusions (Fig. 92). Apparently on the soldier's coat, as no piece of paper is visible, are the words 'Milicia / Bill'. This refers to a Bill of 1757 for conscripting men into the army (the militia) which, it was reported, had resulted in some men who had already served once being drafted for a second term of duty. The man escorting the idiot now has a booklet in his pocket inscribed 'The 6th / Letter to the / . . . / by that' which identifies him as Dr John Shebbeare (1709–88) who had been imprisoned for his attacks on the Marriage Act and who in late 1757 published an attack on the House of Hanover entitled *A Sixth Letter to the People of England*, for which he was again imprisoned. The sick man's election rosette in his cap is enlarged and is now inscribed 'TRUE BLUE'. Hogarth was helped in this engraving by François Morellon de la Cave, who had worked in Amsterdam before coming to London.

The whole scene recalls Horace Walpole's description of the government crisis of 1741 when at each division in Parliament every vote counted. 'It was a most shocking sight', he wrote 'to see the sick and the dead brought in on both sides! . . . men on crutches! and Sir William Gordon from his bed, with a blister on his head, and flannel hanging out from under his wig.'

92. *An Election* III, engraving, third state

SCENE IV: CHAIRING THE MEMBER

This painting shows the successful Tory candidates being carried, or 'chaired', through the streets in triumph (Fig. 93). The shadow of one of them is seen on the wall of the town hall in the background but the other is the centre of a complex group in the foreground. He leans back in alarm as he suddenly comes face to face with the skull and crossbones decorating one of the gateposts to the churchyard, made even more horrifying by the pair of spectacles held in front of the skull by one of the two black chimney-sweeps, wearing blue Tory rosettes in their caps (Fig. 94 detail). The inclusion of the sweeps refers back to the real life incident on Magdalen Bridge described on p. 59. The message of mortality is reinforced by the sundial on the wall of the church which bears the date 1755 and the words 'PULVIS ET UMBRA SUMUS' – we are but dust and shadows. The candidate has more reason for alarm than he realises: in the foreground a one-legged sailor and a rustic are fighting fiercely and the latter has swung his flail back so wildly that he has hit one of the bearers carrying the chair; he is about to collapse and precipitate the new Member of Parliament to the ground. The sailor's performing bear takes advantage of his master's inattention and investigates the barrels of offal on the back of a donkey. The donkey is unperturbed and pauses to eat a thistle while his master raises his stick to strike him. The sailor's other pet, a monkey wearing a coat and a gun, clings to the bear's back and seems alarmed at the turmoil and by being drenched from a source prudently concealed by the capping of the gate pier. The blind fiddler who leads the procession continues unaware of what has happened and seems entirely engrossed in his music. A charging sow and her litter cause even more confusion as they rush towards the stream, presumably an allusion to the madness of the Gadarene swine, which drowned themselves, possessed by demons cast out by Christ. One woman has already been knocked down by their charge. Behind the churchyard wall a well-dressed young girl seems overcome by the confusion and is being tended by an old woman helped by a black lady. Over the new

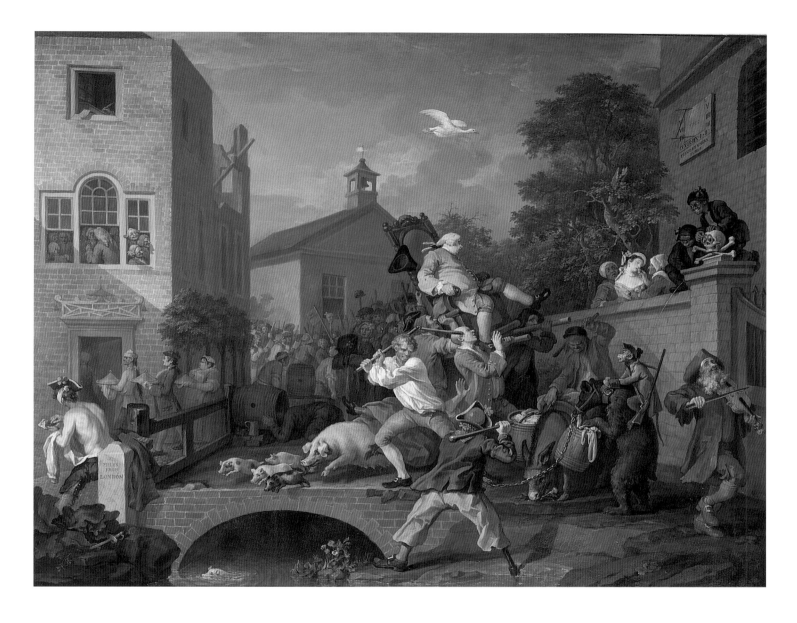

93. *An Election* IV: *Chairing the Member*

Member's head flies a goose. This is said to be an allusion to Le Brun's celebrated painting *The Battle of Arbela* (1669), in the Louvre (Fig. 95) which shows Alexander the Great riding in triumph with a great eagle over his head. Here Hogarth emphasizes the hubris of the scene by replacing the eagle with a goose. The candidate is said to be a portrait of George Bubb Dodington (1690/91–1762), the only prominent Whig to lose a seat (one that he had held for 30 years) in the 1754 election. The Tory procession stretches into the background; blue favours are prominent and a banner reads 'OLD INTEREST'. A woman wearing a Whig favour strikes out at a man (a tailor judging by the scissors), who wears a Tory favour and who turns away protecting his face.

On the left, behind a milestone inscribed 'XI . . . [the rest of the number is not clear] / MILES / FROM / LONDON', a soldier stripped to the waist is refreshing himself with some tobacco from a piece of paper on which is written '. . . ton^s, Best'. He has presumably taken off his shirt and coat to engage in a fight, as he has a bloody

94. *An Election* IV, detail

bandage around his head. In the building on the left, which strangely combines a Palladian window with a Chinese decoration over the door, the losing Whig party are meeting. Some seem disturbed but others are amused by the impending downfall of the member being chaired. The figure wearing the blue ribbon of a decoration may be the Duke of Newcastle. In the window above, a hand can be seen writing. Ireland describes the three figures carrying dishes into the building as 'a half-starved French cook, a half-bred English cook and a half-roasted woman cook'. The figure crawling into the barrel seems to be trying to extract the last dregs.

In fact there was no triumphal procession in Oxford in 1754 as the Tory victory was immediately challenged by the Whigs who made allegations of dubious voter qualifications. Eventually the Sheriff of Oxford took the unusual (and technically illegal) step of returning all four candidates as MPs, leaving Parliament to decide. It was no surprise given the Whig-dominance of the House, that the Whig candidates were duly elected.

The painting is one of Hogarth's masterpieces of composition and one of his most complex; he manages to suggest confusion and chaos but never loses control. Hogarth

95. After Charles Le Brun, *The Battle of Arbela*, engraving.
(© Copyright the Trustees of The British Museum)

96. Peter Paul Rubens, *Battle of the Amazons*
c. 1618–20, oil on panel.
(Bayerische Staatsgemäldesammlungen, Alte
Pinakothek, Munich)

alludes to a range of celebrated artistic precedents. As well as the Le Brun reference, the positioning of the conflict on the brink of a bridge may owe something to Rubens's *The Battle of the Amazons* (Fig. 96). As in the *Election Entertainment* the riotous, almost grotesque, action is contrasted with elegant and exquisite details, to rival any Dutch still life, for example in the depiction of the delicate flowers growing beneath the bridge. This final scene has a strongly meditative quality: at the moment of his success the candidate not only suffers an ignominious fall but is confronted by his own mortality. Hogarth is aiming to convey much more than a passing response to a particular campaign.

The first (proof) state of the engraving of *Chairing the Member* has most of the central group only roughly etched in and lacks all the lettering (Fig. 97). The engravings are close to the painting except that they omit the motif of the drenching of the monkey and, from the second state onwards, this is replaced by the gun on the monkey's back firing inadvertently at the chimney-sweeps (see Fig. 94). This amplifies the reference (see p. 59) to the occasion when an angry Tory mob attacked a post-chaise during the campaign and one of its occupants, Captain Turton, fired at the mob and killed one of its leaders, a chimney-sweep. The inscription placed on the sundial in the second state is 'WE MUST' and is presumably to be read as a rebus with the dial on which it is placed as 'We must die all'. The second state also places a coat of arms borne by winged figures in the pediment of the town hall, and inscribes the banner in the background 'TRUE BLUE' rather than 'OLD INTEREST'. The piece of paper hanging from the upper window has a seal attached.

Apart from the changes noted above, the second state also changes the expression on the candidate's face to anger rather than alarm. The inscription on the milestone is added but is not very clear. Some drapery is hung over the wall in front of the fainting woman. The third state adds the word 'INDINTUR' to the paper with the seal, perhaps suggesting the involvement of lawyers with the election (Fig. 98).

97. *An Election* IV, engraving, first state. (The Royal Collection © 2007, Her Majesty Queen Elizabeth II)

98. *An Election* IV, engraving, third state

Sir John Soane and Hogarth

By the beginning of the nineteenth century Soane was established as a leading architect through his work at the Bank of England, where his original interpretation of neo-classicism was given full reign. His own house at 13 Lincoln's Inn Fields was intended as a celebration of his architectural ideas and as a home for his collection, which included sculpture, casts, architectural models and architectural fragments. He continued to collect works of art until his death in 1837.

As a collector of paintings Soane was interested in encouraging British artists by commissioning works from his contemporaries and purchasing works by founders of the British School. Paintings by non-British artists form only a small part of his collection and he may have favoured Hogarth because he had showed such perseverance in promoting British art. Hogarth was not universally admired at this period but most commentators had few reservations about his satirical dramatic works such as *A Rake's Progress*; in his *Discourses* Sir Joshua Reynolds criticised Hogarth's attempts at the Grand Style but admitted that he had 'invented a new species of dramatick painting, in which probably he will never be equalled'. Soane would have agreed with the 1802 sale catalogue which said of *A Rake's Progress* that 'We speak with Confidence of the Merit of these Paintings; and our Congratulations are ready, to greet the Amateur of Taste and Feeling, who may distinguish himself by securing so enviable a Purchase.' However, *The Gentleman's Magazine* noted the 'want of zeal in the Bidding Cognoscenti' at the *Rake* auction.[26] On 2 March (a few days after the sale on 27 February) Sir George Beaumont offered to buy the *Rake* paintings from Soane but offered only 600 guineas (Soane had paid 679 at the sale).[27] The diarist Joseph Farington, who made the offer on Beaumont's behalf, noted that 'Soane said if He parted with them it must be at a high price'. It was on the engravings that the fame of Hogarth's series rested and the paintings were not much seen or widely valued – even when put on show in 1814 they were not thought to add anything to the engravings. David Bindman has pointed out that the engravings, which could be 'read' in the same way as novels, belonged to the world of literature, periodicals and illustrations rather than to the walls of a gallery of art. Hogarth was seen 'not as an artist in the modern sense but as a moral author whose visual skills enabled him to communicate with a wide audience', ranging from the wealthy and educated to the urban poor.[28]

By acquiring the eight paintings of *A Rake's Progress*, slightly counter to the fashion of the time, Soane may have wished to identify himself with Beckford and other collectors as a patron of the British School of painting.

In buying *An Election*, twenty years later, Soane would have particularly appreciated the connection with David Garrick, generally considered the greatest British actor of the time. Soane was a keen theatre-goer and made substantial donations to theatrical funds. He venerated Shakespeare, creating a 'Shakespeare Recess' on his staircase in

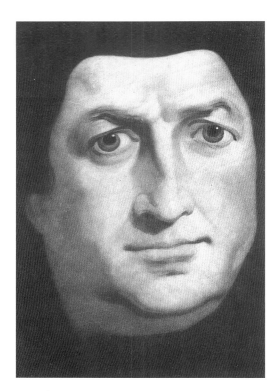

99. Robert Edge Pine, *David Garrick's Death Mask*, mezzotint

tribute to the bard, perhaps inspired by Garrick's own 'Shakespeare Temple' at Hampton. Soane owned a beautifully bound four-volume set of Shakespeare from Garrick's library as well as a proof engraving *Garrick in the Green Room* and a mezzotint by Robert Edge Pine after Garrick's death mask, with eyes added (Fig. 99; Soane believed this showed *Garrick as Cardinal Wolsey*). In his *Analysis of Beauty*, Hogarth commented that 'Shakespeare, . . . has sum'd up all the charms of beauty in two words, INFINITE VARIETY.' Soane also believed that variety was the essence of beauty, seeking to create in his own architecture sequences of varied effects 'which constitute the poetry of architecture.'

Soane may also have felt a kinship with Hogarth because of his association with the Foundling Hospital in Coram's Fields. This institution caught the public imagination during Hogarth's lifetime and became a popular charity: Hogarth had a personal rapport with its founder Captain Thomas Coram and, as a childless man, was touched by the plight of the foundlings. After donating a portrait of the founder, Thomas Coram, in 1740, Hogarth astutely saw that the Hospital's buildings could become a meeting place for London society and conceived the idea of making them a showcase for contemporary British art. He persuaded other artists to present works to the institution and it became a focal point for the artistic community in London until public exhibitions of contemporary art began with the Society of Arts in 1760. In the 1800s, Soane and his wife were themselves frequent visitors to the Foundling Hospital where they would have seen some of Hogarth's grandest works.

Soane's interest in Hogarth is shown by the number of books on the artist in his library (see Bibliography p. 72) as well as by the paintings he purchased. He had a genuine admiration for Hogarth's satirical works, acquiring sets of his engravings as published in the three volumes of John Ireland's *Hogarth Illustrated*, 1791–98, and the two volumes of Samuel Ireland's *Graphic Illustrations of Hogarth*, 1794–99. As an entirely self-made man Soane seems to have identified himself with the industrious apprentice of Hogarth's *Industry and Idleness* series of engravings of 1747. In the dedication of his *Description* of his house and museum, published in 1832, Soane wrote that the book was an 'attempt . . . to show the almost certain successful results of industry and perseverance, so forcibly illustrated in two well-known series of prints by that great moral British artist, William Hogarth'. Soane might, sadly, by this stage of his life have seen parallels between the life of his son, George Soane and that of Hogarth's *Idle Apprentice* or even of his Rake.

In 1827 the first guidebook to Soane's collections, *The Union of Architecture, Sculpture and Painting*, written by his friend the antiquarian John Britton, was published. Britton's description of Soane's two series of Hogarths surely encapsulates Soane's view of them:

> Among the [pictures] . . . are the eight justly admired paintings by Hogarth, of the *Rake's Progress*; and four, called the *Election*. These moral, satirical and graphic essays are replete with entertainment and instruction. They are subjects for intense study, not for casual inspection; and, like the profound writings of a Shakspeare [sic], or the vivacious and pregnant productions of a Sterne, they afford an exhaustless theme for perusal and reflection.

Soane acquired *A Rake's Progress* at a time when he had recently (1800) purchased a country house and estate at Pitzhanger Manor, Ealing, which he was rebuilding for his own use. It was with his new house in mind that he bought the paintings and he displayed them on the ground floor in a small drawing room, along with works by 'modern masters' which probably included two Turner watercolours.

In 1809 Soane decided to sell Pitzhanger Manor and by 1811 the eight 'Rake' canvases had been moved either to his town house at 12 Lincoln's Inn Fields or to his residence at Chelsea Hospital (where he was Clerk of Works from 1807). In 1813 Soane moved into 13 Lincoln's Inn Fields, which he had rebuilt for himself, but he retained the rear part of 12 Lincoln's Inn Fields which was then a library; in 1819 this was converted into a Picture Room and from that date it seems that *A Rake's Progress* hung there in a place of honour on the north wall (Fig. 100).

In October 1823 Soane purchased 14 Lincoln's Inn Fields and built a new Picture Room on the rear part during the following year. The purchase of No. 14 and the creation of the new gallery may have been partly as a direct result of his acquisition of the four large *Election* paintings earlier in 1823: he certainly could not have

100. *A Rake's Progress* displayed in Soane's first Picture Gallery behind 12 Lincoln's Inn Fields. From Britton and Pugin, *Illustrations of the Public Buildings of London*, 1825

accommodated them easily elsewhere. He may also have been encouraged to create a new Picture Room worthy of his growing collection in response to widespread public debate about the creation of a 'national gallery' and the purchase for the nation, in 1824, of the private collection of John Julius Angerstein to form its founding collection.

As soon as Soane's new Picture Room was completed all twelve Hogarths were placed on display there. The paintings comprising *An Election* still hang in their original positions on the lower part of the north and south planes. Three walls of the room are lined with these movable planes which open up like folding doors or shutters to reveal more paintings within and allow three times more pictures to be displayed in the room than such a small space would normally accommodate. In Soane's time *A Rake's Progress* hung behind the north planes of the Picture Room and so were not visible when the planes were shut. Fig. 101 shows the Picture Room as it was in Soane's lifetime with the south planes open and the first two paintings of *An Election* on the north planes to the right. After Soane's death in 1837 his house and collection were established as a Museum for the benefit of the public by an Act of Parliament, which had been passed in 1833. It was probably concern that *A Rake's Progress* should be in a more easily visible position that led to its removal to the South Drawing Room in 1849, where the eight pictures hung on screens in the centre of the room (Fig. 102). In about 1890 they were returned to the Picture Room but were hung on the east wall above the fireplace, in a position where they are visible at all times except when the north and south planes are open. Figure 2 (p. 8) shows Soane's Picture Room as it looks today, restored to its original colour scheme (1988), with the Hogarths hanging on the walls.

THE DRAWING ROOM

102. The South Drawing Room at Sir John Soane's Museum with *A Rake's Progress* displayed on screens, illustration from *The Graphic* magazine, 1 November 1884

NOTE ON THE FRAMES OF *A RAKE'S PROGRESS* AND *AN ELECTION*

The eight paintings of *A Rake's Progress* are in neo-classical black and gilt frames (see Fig.103) of a late eighteenth-century type, *c*.1770s or later. They are architrave frames of a very simple and restrained design, having an ogee-shaped top edge, a run of pearls or beading, a flat frieze with corner *paterae* in the form of rosettes, and a sight moulding of the ornament known as *rais-de-coeur* or lamb's-tongue. Alderman Beckford, who purchased the paintings from Hogarth, died in 1770 and so it was almost certainly his son, William Beckford, who put the paintings into these frames – perhaps in preparation for hanging them at his new house, Fonthill Abbey.

The frames of *An Election* (see Title Page) are fine examples of mid-eighteenth-century carving, in the Rococo style, almost certainly commissioned by Hogarth himself, or by David Garrick (who was such a close friend that he would presumably have consulted Hogarth about his choice). Little is known about Hogarth's frame-makers and there seems to be only one who is definitely known to have worked for Hogarth – one of the Gosset family. This may have been Gideon Gosset (*fl.* 1744–d.1785) or possibly Isaac Gosset (1713–99). In 1748, six or seven years before he completed the *Election* paintings, Hogarth wrote to Gosset asking for a quotation for framing and hanging his large canvas of *Paul before Felix*, painted for the Hall of Lincoln's Inn. A tentative attribution of the *Election* frames to one of the Gossets would accord with the bold, sculptural and three-dimensional qualities of the frames, which point to a Huguenot carver rather than to an English one.

103. *A Rake's Progress* II, to show the frame

1   *A Rake's Progress* and *An Election* were lent to the International Exhibition at South Kensington in 1862. Although the Trustees of Sir John Soane's Museum agreed to lend them to the Universal Exhibition of 1867 in Paris they were in the end not included because it was decided to restrict the 'Fine Arts' section to pictures created since 1855. They have therefore never travelled abroad and the *Rake* has never left London

2   *The Gentleman's Magazine*, July 1823, p.62

3   Hogarth's *The South Sea Scheme* was his response to the wave of disastrous financial speculation that had just swept England, often referred to as 'the South Sea Bubble'. In order to help eliminate the national debt, the government had sponsored the South Sea company, which put investors' funds into dubious projects (for example, a gold mine in Spanish-ruled Peru). When the 'bubble' burst it cost many people their estates and savings

4   *Before* (outdoor or country scene) and its pair, *After*, 1730–31, are in the Fitzwilliam Museum, Cambridge. *Before* (indoor or city scene) and its pair, *After*, *c.*1731, are in the J Paul Getty Museum, Los Angeles, USA

5   The *Harlot's Levée* painting became Scene III of the series

6   The house of correction in Tothill Fields, Westminster, for prostitutes, bawds, cardsharps and others

7   Paulson, *Hogarth's Graphic Works*, 1989, p.76 cites their identification by Dr Brian Allen. They were included in an exhibition at the Cini Foundation in Venice in 1989 (see catalogue, in Italian only, *William Hogarth. Dipinti, disegni, incisioni* (ed. Mary Webster), Grafica Veneta 6, Editore Neri Pozza, Vicenza, 1989)

8   Soane owned a copy of the subscription ticket which hangs in his Dressing Room (SM P21)

9   *London Journal*, 2 November 1734, quoted in Paulson, 1989, p.89

10 Christopher Woodward, 'William Beckford and Fonthill Splendens: early works by Soane and Goodridge', *Apollo*, 432, 1998, pp. 31–40

11 Paulson, 1989, p.114

12 The titles used for the six scenes of *Marriage A-la Mode* are those used by Hogarth in his printed *Proposals* dated 25 January 1745 which announced the sale of the six paintings (in fact he did not actually sell them until 1751)

13 Judy Egerton, *Hogarth's Marriage A-la-Mode*, National Gallery Publications, 1997

14 The meaning of this scene has always been ambiguous. Martin Postle in 'Hogarth's "Marriage a-la-Mode" Scene III: a re-inspection of "The Inspection"', *Apollo*, 429, 1997 suggests that the misconception that sex with a child could cure venereal disease may be implicit in the Viscount's protests

15 *The London Evening Post* 30 April – 2 May 1754

16 Some time after April when John Courtney reported seeing the *Election* paintings in Hogarth's studio: see Paulson, *Hogarth*, 1993, Vol. III, p.367

17 This story is recorded in Farington's Diary, 7 March 1802

18 The painting is in Tate Britain, London

19 William Hogarth to Hester Thrale, in *Anecdotes of Samuel Johnson*, 1786

20 The unusual sprawled pose of the Rake in this scene seems to have been influenced by a French engraving by Francois-Bernard Lépicié after Watteau, *Antoine de la Roque*, 1732 (Robin Simon, '*Un rosbif à Paris*: Hogarth's visit to Paris in 1743', *British Art Journal*, Volume VII, No. 2, Autumn 2006, pp. 24–33)

21 Leather Coat was used, as Leathersides, by Fielding as a character in *The Covent Garden Tragedy*, 1732. See Paulson, 1989, p.94

22 Paulson, 1989, p.94 makes the point that Tom will be, literally, 'burnt up' in Scene VIII by the syphilis he has caught from the prostitutes

23 *The London Magazine* May 1754, p.212

24 A 17th-century tune used by John Gay as the opening Air in his popular *Beggar's Opera*, 1729

25 Handel's dramatic cantata, *The Choice of Hercules*, written in a similar verse form, was first performed in London in 1751

26 *The Gentleman's Magazine*, March 1802, p.218

27 This incident is recorded in Farington's Diary, 2 March 1802

28 See David Bindman, 'The fame of "A Rake's Progress": The paintings and the prints' in Robin Simon and Christopher Woodward (eds), *A Rake's Progress. From Hogarth to Hockney.* Exhibition catalogue, Sir John Soane's Museum, 1997

BIBLIOGRAPHY

These books were in Soane's library

Anon., *An Explanation of the Eight Prints of The Rake's Progress copied from the Originals of Mr William Hogarth, according to the Act of Parliament*; by Thomas Bakewell, Printseller, next Johnson's Court, London, 1735

Anon., *A Rake's Progress or The Humours of Drury Lane. A Poem*, London, 1735

Anon., *The Humours of a Country Election*, London, 1741

Anon., *A Practical Description of Mr. Hogarth's Election Prints in Four Cantos. Written under Mr. Hogarth's Sanction and Inspection*, London, 1759

Antal, Frederick, *Hogarth and his Place in European Art*, London, 1962

Beckett, R B, *Hogarth*, London, 1949

Bindman, David, *Hogarth*, London, 1981

Bindman, David, *Hogarth and his Times: Serious Comedy*. Catalogue of an exhibition at the British Museum, 1997–98

Bindman, David, Ekserdjian, David and Palin, Will eds, *Hogarth's Election Entertainment. Artists at the Hustings*. Catalogue of an exhibition at Sir John Soane's Museum, 2001

Bindman, David, Ogée, Frédéric and Wagner, Peter, *Hogarth: representing nature's machines*, Manchester, 2001

Bindman, David and Wilcox, Scott, *"Among the Whores and Thieves", William Hogarth and The Beggar's Opera*. Catalogue of an exhibition at the Yale Center for British Art, New Haven, 1997

Cowley, Robert L S, *William Hogarth and His Dogs*, The Antique Collector, October 1987

Cowley, Robert L S, *Marriage A-la-Mode: a re-view of Hogarth's narrative art*, Manchester, 1983

Dabydeen, David, *Hogarth's Blacks. Images of Blacks in Eighteenth Century English Art*, Manchester, 1987

Egerton, Judy, *Hogarth's Marriage A-la-Mode*. Published to accompany an exhibition at The National Gallery, 1997–98

Einberg, Elizabeth, *Hogarth the Painter*. Catalogue of an exhibition at the Tate Gallery, 1997

Einberg, Elizabeth, *Manners and Morals: Hogarth and British Painting 1700–1760*. Catalogue of Tate Gallery Exhibition, 1987–88

Farington, Joseph, *The Diary of Joseph Farington*, Garlick, Kenneth and Macintyre, Alistair eds vols 1-6; Cave, Kathryn ed. vols 7–14; Newby, Evelyn ed. Index, New Haven and London, 1978–98

Fielding, Henry, * *Pasquin*, 1736

Gowing, Lawrence, *Hogarth*. Catalogue of Tate Gallery Exhibition, 1971–72

Hallett, Mark and Riding, Christine, *Hogarth*, Exhibition Catalogue, Tate, 2006

Hogarth, William, * *The Analysis of Beauty* (1753), ed. Joseph Burke, Oxford, 1955

Hogarth, William, *Autobiographical Notes*, in *The Analysis of Beauty*, ed. Joseph Burke, Oxford, 1955

Hogarth, William, *Apology for Painters*, ed. Michael Kitson, *Walpole Society*, Vol. XLI, Oxford 1968, pp. 46–111

Ireland, John, *Hogarth Illustrated*, 3 vols, London, 1791–98

Ireland, Samuel, *Graphic Illustrations of Hogarth*, 2 vols, London, 1794–99

Kunzle, David, *Plagiaries by Memory of A Rake's Progress*, Journal of the Warburg and Courtauld Institutes, Vol. XXIX, 1966

Kurz, Hilde, *Italian Models of Hogarth's Picture Series*. Journal of the Warburg and Courtauld Institutes. Vol. XV 3–4 1952

Mitchell, Charles, ed., *Hogarth's Peregrination*, Oxford, 1952

Moore, Robert E, *Hogarth's Literary Relationships*, Minneapolis, 1948

Nichols, John, Steevens, George, Reed, Isaac, and others, *Biographical Anecdotes of William Hogarth*, London, 1781, 1782, 1785

Nichols, John, and Steevens, George, *The Genuine Works of William Hogarth*, 3 vols, London, 1808–17

Nichols, J B, *Anecdotes of William Hogarth*, London, 1833

Oppé, A P, *The Drawings of William Hogarth*, London, 1948

Paulson, Ronald, *Hogarth's Graphic Works: First Complete Edition*, 2 vols, New Haven, 1965; revised ed., 1970; third revised ed., 1989

Paulson, Ronald, *Hogarth: His Life, Art and Times*, 2 vols, New Haven and London, 1971

Paulson, Ronald, *Hogarth*. 3 vols, New Brunswick, 1991–93

Piozzi, H L., *Anecdotes of the late Samuel Johnson*, London, 1786

Postle, Martin, 'In search of the "True Briton": Reynolds, Hogarth and the British School' in Allen, Brian (ed.) *Towards a Modern Art World (Studies in British Art)*, Yale University Press, 1992

Quennell, Peter, *Hogarth's Progress*, New York, 1955

Robson, J R, *The Oxfordshire Election of 1754*, London, 1949

Rouquet, Jean André, *Lettres de Monsieur** à un de ses Amis a Paris*, London, 1746

Rouquet, Jean Andre, * *State of the Arts in England*, London, 1755

Simon, Robin and Woodward, Christopher eds, *A Rake's Progress. From Hogarth to Hockney*. Catalogue of an exhibition at Sir John Soane's Museum, 1997

Simon, Robin, *Hogarth, France and British Art*, London, 2007

Taggart, Ross E, *A Tavern Scene: An Evening at the Rose (Study for scene III of the Rake's Progress)*, Art Quarterly XIX, 1956

Trusler, J, *The Country Election, A Farce*, London, 1768

Tharp, Lars, *Hogarth's China. Hogarth's Paintings and 18th-Century Ceramics*, London, 1997

Uglow, Jenny, *Hogarth A Life and a World*, London, 1997

Walpole, Horace, *Anecdotes of Painting in England*, IV (1771, released 1780), ed. James Dallaway, London, 1828

Waterhouse, Ellis, *Painting in England, 1530 to 1790*, London, 1953

Whitley, W T, *Artists and their Friends in England, 1700-1799*, 2 vols, London, 1928

Wind, E, *Borrowed Attitudes in Reynolds and Hogarth*, Journal of the Warburg Institute, Vol. 2, 1938–39